Christophe André is the bestselling author of many books, including the internationally acclaimed *Mindfulness: 25 ways to live in the moment through art*. One of France's leading psychiatrists, he works at the Sainte-Anne Hospital in Paris, where he helps people to free themselves from emotional problems such as anxiety and depression through the use of mindfulness and positive psychology.

HAPPINESS

25 ways to live joyfully through art

CHRISTOPHE ANDRÉ

Translated by Trista Selous

LONDON · SYDNEY · AUCKLAND · JOHANNESBURG

1 3 5 7 9 10 8 6 4 2

Rider, an imprint of Ebury Publishing,
20 Vauxhall Bridge Road,
London SW1V 2SA

Rider is part of the Penguin Random House group of companies whose addresses
can be found at global.penguinrandomhouse.com

Copyright © Christophe André 2014
English translation copyright © Trista Selous 2016

Christophe André has asserted his right to be identified as the author of this Work
in accordance with the Copyright, Designs and Patents Act 1988

This edition first published in the Great Britain by Rider Books in 2016
Originally published in France as *De l'art du bonheur* by L'Iconoclaste, Paris in 2014

www.penguin.co.uk

A CIP catalogue record for this book is available from the British Library

ISBN 97818460445059

Printed and bound in Italy by L.E.G.O. S.p.A

Penguin Random House is committed to a sustainable future for our business,
our readers and our planet. This book is made from Forest Stewardship Council®
certified paper.

*To André Comte-Sponville
with warmth and gratitude.*

*In memory of Aleth and to Rémy
for the moments of happiness and
sadness spent together.*

HAPPINESS
AS A WORK OF ART

'Painting is a ceremony in solitude,' wrote the philosopher Alain. Is it my work as a psychiatrist, my fondness for silence and my interest in the personal and emotional that draws me to painting and its power to affect us? I can't say. But I would like to help readers explore the benefits of looking at a painting, breathing gently, saying nothing and letting the picture speak and live within us – making space for it within us.

In this book the faces, forms and flow of happiness are embodied in twenty-five masterpieces. These paintings encourage us to feel, meditate and reflect. They also offer twenty-five 'lessons' to help us develop our capacity for happiness.

Some of these painters of happiness had happy lives, others were unhappy for long periods. But all were drawn to the idea of happiness and its *necessity*. Even the most fulfilled among them were aware that happiness is fleeting and hard to find, and that having appeared it inevitably fades.

For happiness is a living emotion, which is born, grows, blossoms, fades and vanishes. It goes in cycles, just as night follows day. This natural rhythm will be our guiding thread through the masterpieces in this book, which depict mornings, middays, dusks and nights of happiness – and also, of course, its endless rebirth.

'THERE ARE MANY WHO SAY,
WHO WILL SHOW US ANY GOOD?'

PSALM 4, OLD TESTAMENT

PRELUDE
THE ENIGMA
OF HAPPINESS

W e've been searching so long for happiness that we may even come to doubt its existence or the point of pursuing it. So we get on with our ordinary lives, neither totally sad nor totally happy, until once again we sense the existence of happiness like a question to be answered, an imperious mystery to be solved.

The geographer in Vermeer's painting is trying to solve an enigma of a different kind – perhaps it is the mystery of Paradise. Well into the seventeenth

The Geographer
Johannes Vermeer (1632–1675)
1688, oil on canvas, 52 x 45.5 cm, Städelsches Kunstinstitut, Frankfurt-am-Main.

In the period when Vermeer painted this picture, science had just undergone a fundamental transformation. Until this time, conducting research into the nature of the stars, the Earth or life itself had been seen as contrary to the Divine plan. A mere thirty years before, Galileo had been condemned for his discoveries and forced, on his knees, to deny that the Earth goes round the sun. But by the seventeenth century scientific 'curiositas' was no longer banned by the religious authorities or censured by conservative humanists.

Today's scientific research into happiness arouses ironic responses from some clerics, but this irony is unfounded and spurious. Knowing the chemical formula of a rose's scent doesn't make it less exquisite or poetic.

century many people still believed that Paradise might be somewhere on Earth, and many speculated as to the most likely location – the Middle East maybe, or South America. Though centuries have passed since then, the geographer's quest is similar to our own. In the closed space of his room he is trying to make a map of the world, and we do the same in our thinking about happiness, based on our personal experiences.

People have always searched for happiness. The Greeks adopted it as the first goal of philosophy more than two thousand years ago. The word *eudaimonia*, Aristotle's highest human good, is usually translated as 'happiness'. The aim of Greek philosophy was to help human beings attain happier lives. Today, scientists have been taking a keen interest in happiness for some years – they refer to it by the less poetic appellation of 'subjective well-being'. In their eyes this well-being is good for us in many different ways, from increasing longevity and improving health to making us more altruistic.

Artists too have talked of happiness and also unhappiness, its unavoidable shadow. Poets, writers and musicians have created works that make us weep and then suddenly make us feel light-hearted, confident and happy. Painters have shown that they can arouse our emotions in more subtle ways, changing our routine, habitual view of reality, moments of happiness and feelings of unhappiness. As we seek to solve the mystery of happiness, painting can act as our enigmatic guide, speaking to us only through images and metaphors, beyond words and reason.

Our geographer too is pursuing an enigma. For a long time he has been thinking, calculating, finding answers, changing his mind and realising he has gone in the wrong direction. Now he lifts his head to the light, letting his gaze leave the room and slip out of the window – which is on the left of the picture, as always in Vermeer's paintings. Our geographer has done enough thinking. He has a feeling that science, work and intelligence are no longer enough. He has realised that for his quest to succeed he must now allow something else to emerge within him, something like intuition, or emotion. He has a sense that the solution to the question that has been plaguing him is not to be found outside, in maps, globes or the points of his compasses, but within. At this point in history, when human beings were gradually abandoning the belief that Paradise was on Earth or in the heavens, Vermeer's geographer has a vague feeling that the Paradise whose path he seeks in fact lies within himself.

'I HAVE STRIVEN NOT TO LAUGH AT HUMAN ACTIONS,
NOT TO WEEP AT THEM, NOR TO HATE THEM,
BUT TO UNDERSTAND THEM.'
SPINOZA

MORNING
THE BIRTH
OF HAPPINESS

POWERFUL AND FRAGILE, LIKE LIFE ITSELF
Van Gogh, Branch with Almond Blossom

OUR EARLIEST HAPPINESS
Klimt, The Three Ages of Woman

THE HAPPINESS OF CHILDHOOD
Monet, The Artist's Garden at Vétheuil

EVERYDAY HAPPINESS
Fragonard, The Cascatelle at Tivoli

POWERFUL AND FRAGILE, LIKE LIFE ITSELF

Soaring into the blue, almond blossom stretches up to the sky. Here we see only the white of the petals and the azure above, like an embodiment of happiness, as powerful and fragile as life itself. Exhausted by inner chaos and his struggle with mental illness, Van Gogh magnificently cuts to what matters most – life's upward impulse towards the heavens and transcendence. He painted this picture with his head lifted to the sky, seeing nothing else around him. He has shut out the landscape and all other details, right down to the trunk of the tree, in order to concentrate on the union of sky and blossom – opposing poles of blue and white, ephemeral and eternal, earthly and heavenly.

In the same way, he has kept out – though not denied – his sufferings of the moment, in order to give us a lasting expression of the happiness he feels at the sight of almond blossom.

'MAN IS BORN TO BE HAPPY, SO ALL OF NATURE TEACHES.'

ANDRÉ GIDE

Branch with Almond Blossom
Vincent Van Gogh (1853–1890)

1890, oil on canvas, 73.5 x 92 cm, Van Gogh Museum, Vincent Van Gogh Foundation, Amsterdam.

When he painted this picture in February 1890, in the asylum of Saint-Rémy-de-Provence where he had sought refuge, Van Gogh was very ill. His life was dominated by periods of insanity that left him exhausted. In July of the same year he shot himself in the chest. And yet 31 January had seen the birth in Paris of another Vincent, son of the painter's older brother Theo and to whom he was godfather. The picture was painted for this baby, whose new life was just beginning, like almond blossom bursting up towards the sky at the end of winter.

In May, Van Gogh left Provence and went to Auvers-sur-Oise, where he was treated by Dr Gachet. Passing through Paris, he stopped off to visit his godson and give him this gift. On seeing the baby in the cradle, the adult Vincent was moved to tears.

This painting and the ode to nature it conveys reflect Van Gogh's sense of wonder at the infinite generosity of creation: 'In my case the emotions that take hold of me in the face of nature go as far as fainting, and then the result is a fortnight during which I am incapable of working.'

Van Gogh's Lesson:
LOOK UP TO THE SKY

Sequi naturam, 'follow nature'. The Ancient philosophers understood very well that there is an organic link between nature and happiness. No doubt this is why human beings have always imagined Paradise as a garden rather than a palace. Etymologically, the word 'paradise' comes from the Persian *pari-deza*, which became *paradeisos* in Greek and refers to a walled oasis, protected from the burning desert winds. Happiness is so fragile. Nature helps us understand happiness and brings us closer to it in many different ways. It offers us a peaceful, ancestral connection to the complex world around us through the unending cycle of seasons, the seemingly changeless landscapes that we love and the harmonious interconnectedness of animals and plants. It teaches us not to expect anything in particular, but just to be there and enjoy it.

Nature creates harmony through connection and belonging. When we feel simply that we are alive among all other forms of life, and understand that we are lucky to be so, we taste the fundamental happiness of being alive.

For evolutionary psychologists, many aspects of our behaviour and the things that attract us are traces of the needs we had as animals. Human beings take such pleasure from looking at the beauties of nature – a tree-lined river or sun-drenched shoreline – because they see in them the promise of resources for their survival, such as food, somewhere to rest and recover. Yet, beyond the sense of pleasure there is also an obscure, deep sense of belonging to an order much greater than us and which we are part of. More than simply observing or even admiring nature, we become complicit with it, sensing our most basic identity as living things. When we look at a tree in blossom, or lose ourselves in the movement of waves and clouds, we become part of nature, we return to it.

Every time we breathe in the scent of fields or forest, the happiness we feel is the inner echo of our biological roots. These encounters with nature do more than simply foster happiness – they are indispensable to it.

'I GOT UP IN THE NIGHT
TO LOOK AT THE LANDSCAPE –
NEVER, NEVER HAS NATURE APPEARED
SO TOUCHING AND SO SENSITIVE TO ME.'
VINCENT VAN GOGH

Van Gogh's painting could have been called 'The Birth of Happiness', because it has all the fragility and power of human joys, their rootedness in life and drive for transcendence. These emerging joys are at once extremely important and extremely vulnerable. It is so easy for them to be trampled on or neglected. This painting opens our eyes to their beauty and fragility, and to their absolute necessity to our lives.

Happiness as a whole is born in such moments of grace. Stand still and be silent. Look, listen, breathe. Admire. Make room for happiness to emerge. Gently work on perceiving it wherever it appears. This is the first and most fundamental lesson.

'AS I WALKED LATE IN THE EVENING
DOWN THIS TREE-LINED AVENUE,
A CHESTNUT FELL AT MY FEET.
THE SOUND IT MADE AS IT BURST OPEN,
ITS ECHO WITHIN ME AND A SHOCK
OUT OF ALL PROPORTION WITH THIS TINY EVENT,
PLUNGED ME INTO THE MIRACLE,
THE INTOXICATION OF THE DEFINITIVE,
AS THOUGH THERE WERE NO LONGER ANY
QUESTIONS, ONLY ANSWERS.'

ÉMILE CIORAN

OUR EARLIEST
HAPPINESS

A child snuggles up to her mother, both asleep in a touching, tender embrace. Lying against her mother's slender breast the child seems to be absorbing all she can of the woman who has given her life, warmth and love. As always in Klimt's art, dreamlike decorative motifs combine with hyperrealist detail. See how the child's extended little finger presses against the soft warmth of her mother's skin. Look at her rumpled, tangled hair,

The Three Ages of Woman
Gustav Klimt (1862–1918)
*1905, oil on canvas, 178 x 198 cm,
Galleria nazionale d'arte moderna, Rome.*

In Klimt's work the world has a woman's face. Femininity is everywhere in his art, always sensual, often mysterious and sometimes terrifying. Klimt himself was taciturn, sometimes to the point of rudeness, and described by friends and family as an awkward man, a loner with little interest in social duties and commercial requirements, who found happiness only in work. Of himself he said, 'I don't think I am particularly interesting as a person.' We know his relationships with women produced three children. Emilie Flöge, his muse and life-long companion, said of him, 'A true artist lives only for his work ... Klimt was a slow artist ... That was why he needed this tenacious, flamboyant enthusiasm as a distraction.'

plastered against her forehead by the hot dampness of sleep. Her head is turned to the side, against her shoulder, so she can be even closer to her mother. See how, as the child absorbs, the mother protects. The position of her head looks uncomfortable, but it shelters the child she holds with her slender arm. She is nourishing her little one with love, heart against heart, and this child, against whose head she rests her own, is also her own past and future.

Klimt's painting helps us think about the great mystery that is the birth of happiness, and the way that we pass on and prepare for the happiness to come. The happiness depicted here is at once a legacy and a promise.

'HAPPINESS,
AN ANIMAL IDEA ...'
PAUL VALÉRY

KLIMT'S LESSON:
LOVE BEING HAPPY

Finding happiness is perhaps simply a matter of rediscovering it. The birth of that complex, furtive feeling we call 'happiness' may lie in our most distant memories.

Today we know that human beings cannot do without emotional nourishment. When children are deprived of love they die, either physically or psychologically. When they are neglected they suffer, and the adults they later become have difficulty finding happiness. It seems that being happy means rediscovering and awakening the memory of past happiness, and in particular our very earliest happiness at being loved and protected. It's like an early imprint of happiness.

In psychology, theories of imprinting reveal that there are times in our lives when we are best able to learn certain things. Take languages, for example: languages that we have heard often and early are easier for us to learn. In the same way, the language of happiness is

'WHERE DO WE GET THIS
NOTION OF HAPPINESS FROM?
IF IT LIES IN OUR MEMORY,
THAT MUST MEAN WE WERE HAPPY
IN THE PAST.'

SAINT AUGUSTINE

more accessible to us if we experienced it in infancy – if we learned it even before we learned the language of spoken words. And this early learning makes it easier for us to go on learning later. Multilingual people tend to speak several languages because they learned them very young. Why should it not be the same for happiness? What if it is our childhood happiness that later gives us access to all adult forms of happiness? These early, inexpressible imprints contain the beating heart of our future aptitude for happiness and our capacity to feel happy.

If we received this imprint of happiness when we were very young, we were lucky. Our first duty is not to waste it, because we have things to do. But if we have not been so lucky, we must set to work.

We can always learn happiness, even if it was not our mother tongue ...

What is it that enables children to attain happiness once they reach adulthood? In the first place it is almost certainly the memory of happiness, a constellation of memories and feelings from happy times, some vague, some astonishingly detailed. The more dense and numerous these memories, the greater our capacity for happiness will be, knowing that we have a place at the table.

But the capacity to build this happiness does not rely solely on a store of memories. We must also want to do it. As Marcel Proust describes in *In Remembrance of Things Past*, 'Again the dazzling and indistinct vision fluttered near me, as if to say, "Seize me as I pass if you can, and try to solve the riddle of happiness which I set you."' Proust shows us that vague memories are nothing without the desire to make the happy feeling return, as in the more famous episode of the madeleine.

Beyond early imprinting, the capacity for happiness also depends on our willingness to become happy, and to make the effort to do so.

Why do we have this almost animal belief that happiness exists, and that there is nothing crazy or pointless about looking for it? Why do most of us go on stubbornly – sometimes clumsily – searching for it? Why aren't human beings satisfied with all the moments of animal well-being offered us by a life that is materially acceptable – having a full stomach, being warm and enjoying physical pleasures? Why do we have this need for transcendence, for plenitude, which we seek and sometimes find in the feeling of happiness? The answer is also to be found in Klimt's painting. If we expand our field of vision beyond the mother and child, we find a disturbing world of expanses of plain, dark colours, trails of shadow and the ravaged body of an old woman.

Human life is hard and sometimes tragic, for the passing of time always hurts our flesh. Without happiness, without this ability to give meaning to our lives, how could we not sink into depression and despair?

Being happy is a necessity, not a luxury. Happiness is what makes life psychologically possible. We do not live *to be* happy, but *because* we can be happy. As Paul Claudel said: 'Happiness is not the goal of life, but its means.'

'YOU ASK ME WHAT IS THE SUPREME HAPPINESS ON EARTH? IT IS TO LISTEN TO A LITTLE GIRL SINGING AS SHE WALKS INTO THE DISTANCE HAVING ASKED YOU THE WAY.'

LIPO

THE HAPPINESS
OF CHILDHOOD

L ike a memory of happiness – a big garden, a blue sky with passing clouds, games, processions and shouts, big flowers and a mum or dad in the distance, keeping a watchful eye. Light, sounds, smells and details. A little boy gazes at the domesticated nature opening up before him.

In the background are the reassuring, horizontal lines of the house and two familiar figures, his mother and another child. Around him are the vertical lines of the

The Artist's Garden in Vétheuil
Claude Monet (1840–1926)
1881 (dated 1880), oil on canvas, 150 x 120 cm, National Gallery of Art, Washington.

Monet painted several views of his house in Vétheuil shortly before he left it. During his three years there, great sorrows, including the death of his wife Camille, were mixed with great joys, particularly his relationship with his future partner, whose form can be glimpsed at the top of the steps. Alice Hoschédé was married to Monet's patron Ernest. The little boy who is not sure whether to run down the garden is Michel Monet, the painter's son, while the other is almost certainly Jean-Pierre Hoschédé. The two boys had been born a few months apart and were inseparable.

Monet had moored his studio boat on the Seine, below the great avenue in the centre of the painting. And so he moved from one garden to the next – Argenteuil, then Vétheuil, and finally Giverny, where he spent the rest of his life.

sunflowers, like a benevolent jungle, and before him opens the path, which draws him so strongly that it makes him stop for a moment, before rushing ahead.

But is this hesitation about apprehension, or something more subtle, a kind of animal intelligence and intuitive wisdom? Perhaps he is simply savouring this moment of perfect balance between the known and the unknown, stillness and movement, present and future. Let's imagine …

He is completely happy and for him time has stopped. He feels that he has a boundless future, the sense that life will contain infinite happiness, again and again, for ever.

'CHILDREN HAVE NEITHER PAST NOR FUTURE
AND — SOMETHING THAT SELDOM HAPPENS TO US —
THEY ENJOY THE PRESENT.'

LA BRUYÈRE

MONET'S LESSON :
CHILDREN CAN TEACH US A LOT ABOUT HAPPINESS

Children live in the present: they naturally avoid the anticipation and rumination that gnaw at our adult minds. Their experiences of life, however ordinary they may seem, build up an invisible underground reservoir of future happiness, a treasure chest they can draw on later and which will enable them to get through the trials and pains that come their way. Childhood is also the time for learning future happiness. For happiness must be *learned* and, like every form of learning, it starts with copying models. What do Mum and Dad have to show me about the way we enjoy the beauty of life? What do they show me of the way we face adversity?

But let's not idealise childhood happiness. In the future we will never be able to experience it in the same way, with the same spontaneity. It's a mistake to try to return at any price to this original state of grace, or to think that happiness has to be a natural thing that will come if we wait. Why should happiness acquired

'MY WHOLE BODY IS POROUS TO THE COOL WIND OF SPRING. EVERYWHERE I MAKE MYSELF INFINITE AND EVERYWHERE I'M HAPPY. I AM GLAD FOR YESTERDAY, TODAY AND TOMORROW, BELIEVING MYSELF TO BE GOD WITHOUT BEGINNING OR END.'

PAUL FORT

through effort necessarily be inferior or less intense? How naïve to argue this way! Or how lazy.

Another mistake, linked to a different form of pain, is that of reliving our childhood happiness through a mist of nostalgia, and so becoming exiled from it.

We need to feel glad for the past, rather than weep for it. This can be hard when we look back at happiness past, but that's no reason to give up.

Our relationship to happiness is akin to what Monet describes in this painting. It is based on a subtle balance between rootedness and impulse. This little boy pausing before he runs into the garden is a bit like us faced with life itself. Being happy is conceivable only if we are open to the vastness of the world. Happiness cannot survive if we withdraw into ourselves, close ourselves in and shut down. Confinement is never – or seldom – a choice. It is usually dictated by pain or fear and by paths through life that have imposed it on us. Conversely, the instinct of childhood is to set off into the wide world in search of happiness.

But this movement is possible only when we have a base to return to. This is what the psychologists call 'secure attachment'. The degree to which children – and the adults they later become – are able to enjoy exploring the world and life is directly related to how sure they are – from experience – that they have secure bases behind them. This little boy would never run into this imposing garden without such stable moorings, without knowing that his mother and the house will be there to welcome him back from his adventures, and crucially from his potential misadventures. Happiness is not a matter of staying shut up in the house, clinging to our roots. But it can be about returning to them, and knowing they are there when we are far away. They must exist.

We need certainties, however limited, if we are to be able to tolerate the uncertainty of the boundless. We need to be rooted so that we can dare to set off into life. These things are vital to our happiness.

Happiness feeds on a free interplay of the known and the unknown. Both are necessary, as revealed by children and also cats, which we regard as often happy (and maybe we are right), because they seem to us to embody a harmony of sedentariness and independence. Maintaining this balance is the major task of adult happiness. On the one hand there is the temptation to remain safe and still – at the risk of boredom and loss of vitality – on the other that of the frantic quest for the new, with the risk of superficiality and vacuity.

Our hearts strive after happiness. It is up to us to find a balance between the happiness of expansion and that of new beginnings, the happiness of action and that of meditation.

Look at the little boy in the garden. He has resolved his dilemma, and he's off! Hesitation to the winds, he's starting to run, confidently throwing himself into the arms of happiness.

EVERYDAY
HAPPINESS

W omen are busy doing their laundry and hanging it out. Shirts are already drying in the wind. It's a sunny day. In the distance we can see the little waterfalls known as the Cascatelle, which gave their name to the painting and brought fame to the town of Tivoli, near Rome. Fragonard has chosen to show us a scene of everyday life. These women are working.

The Cascatelle at Tivoli
Jean Honoré Fragonard (1732–1806)
c. 1760, oil on canvas, 72 x 60 cm,
Musée du Louvre, Paris.

According to his contemporaries, Fragonard had a particular gift for happiness. His sister-in-law used to say, 'If I wanted to paint the joy, gaiety, whimsy, caresses and happiness of a child, I would take him for model. If I wanted to paint the nature, gentleness, willingness, care and tenderness of friendship, I would again take him for model.'

The Fragonards moved from Provence to Paris with their only son, aged six. 'Good old Frago' worked first in Chardin's studio, and then under Boucher. He was not ambitious for an official career, but was content with the success his light-hearted, graceful paintings obtained among rich clients. He was of that generation of painters who still saw themselves as simple artisans. This makes his genius all the more moving in its spontaneity. Fragonard died poor and neglected, but unhappy? Maybe not …

'I WHO HAVE NO OTHER AIM
BUT TO LIVE AND BE MERRY.'

MICHEL DE MONTAIGNE

They are not princesses but washerwomen, servants or simply mothers. Their homes are not palaces but old dwellings with crumbling walls.

The feeling we have when we look at this little painting, lost among the masterpieces of the Louvre, relates precisely to the ordinariness of what it depicts. This is not happiness striking a pose, but a happy scene that has forgotten to look in the mirror and think about itself. These are ordinary people doing ordinary things. What Fragonard has painted is the possibility of happiness and the conditions that foster its emergence. Simple happiness in moments of simplicity.

FRAGONARD'S LESSON :
PREPARE YOUR MIND
FOR HAPPINESS

If there's no happiness in everyday life, what's the point? What is the point of happiness that arrives only in exceptional circumstances, or comes only to exceptional people? Happiness cannot be *above* everyday moments (perfect, pure happiness) or *alongside* them (happiness as an escape from everyday wretchedness that must be borne). It must be found *within* life itself. For a long time people expected and imagined happiness to lie only in the Beyond of Paradise. Then came the eighteenth century and its wonderful, generous decision to democratise happiness: 'Paradise is where I am.' With the emergence of Voltaire and many others, the happiness of everyday life came into its own.

The feeling of a happy life stems from a succession of little moments of happiness, rather than in a few very great joys. If happiness is like gold, we are far more likely to find it as dust than in nuggets.

'GO THY WAY, EAT THY BREAD WITH JOY,
AND DRINK THY WINE WITH A MERRY HEART.'

OLD TESTAMENT, BOOK OF ECCLESIASTES

Poets and writers have noted the importance of these snatches of happiness as opportunities to be grasped and savoured. Together these fragments form the basis of a happy life. They are small change that we can use to meet our everyday needs for happiness.

The smallness of these moments of happiness does not mean that they don't matter. They do. Firstly, because when frequently repeated they gradually lead us towards a sense of the happiness of life. Secondly, because they reveal the depth in ordinary things, which remains inaccessible to us if we act without feeling. Our receptiveness to happiness also keeps us open to surprise and disorder, which break into our routines to show us that everything is more beautiful than we thought. For every life has a depth that is invisible to the hasty eye. Fragonard's painting discreetly shows us this. Look at the many different planes of which it is made (sky, clouds, waterfalls, wall of greenery, figures) and also the abyss that lies below the figures, suggested by the boy in red in the foreground, leaning over into empty space, and the woman on the terrace, stretching out her arm to point to something. Happiness deepens everything, and sometimes surprises us.

The phrase 'surprised by happiness' sounds great, doesn't it? But how can we let ourselves be *surprised* by happiness? It's not so easy. We need to have spent a long time honing our way of seeing. This was Fragonard's secret.

Let's keep our eyes open to the beauties of everyday life. Let us rejoice at being alive, here and now. These are our first and most frequent opportunities for happiness.

Some say happiness can't be pursued. This may be true, but we can sometimes meet it by chance. Like love, it's one of those strange, subtle states that we can't attain if we wait and hope for them too much. But it takes a little effort all the same. We won't find love if we shut ourselves up at home, or happiness if we focus on our ego. So how can we extract happiness from everyday life without separating the two? Most often, life brings us naturally closer to the sources of happiness through our activities, social relations and harmony with nature. If we are fully engaged with life, happiness will come. But how can we never forget this, without constantly thinking about it?

Let's not turn happiness into an obsession. If we live our lives it will come. But for this to happen, we need to know how to open our eyes to the happiness that doesn't know what it is and that we don't recognise.

In studies and research into happiness, most people questioned spontaneously describe themselves as 'fairly happy'. Is this an illusion? Is it auto-suggestion? Or is it simply wisdom? These people may perhaps not be completely happy at the time of asking, but they intuitively know that happiness can come into their lives at any time, arising out of the states of pre-happiness that regularly appear in our everyday lives. A happy life is not a life in which we *always* feel happy, but one in which we feel that happiness is possible – a fertile life that gives birth to many moments of happiness.

We should not wait for happiness, or think about it all the time, but we should know that it may appear, and prepare for its arrival.

MIDDAY
THE PLENITUDE
OF HAPPINESS

LIKE A FORCE THAT WILL...
Monet, La Rue Montorgueil in Paris

WHAT MAKES FOR HAPPINESS
Chagall, Peasant Life

THE INTELLIGENCE OF HAPPINESS
Chaissac, Figure on a Blue Background

THE BREATH OF LOVE
Friedrich, On the Sailing Boat

ONLY CONNECT
Veronese, Iseppo da Ponto and his Son Adriano

HAPPINESS BEYOND OURSELVES
Giotto, The Gift of the Mantle

LIKE A FORCE
THAT WILL...

t's a beautiful morning in June. In Rue Montorgueil in Paris every window sports at least one tricolour flag flapping proudly in the breeze, lining the buildings with dancing blue, white and red, while the street below is filled with a great crowd. We can tell that the people are joyful, bathed in summer sunlight, filled with the euphoria of this festive, jubilant atmosphere. Monet's painting radiates an extraordinary energy and vitality. The oblique

The Rue Montorgueil in Paris. Celebration of 30 June 1878
Claude Monet (1840–1926)
1878, oil on canvas, 81 x 50 cm, Musée d'Orsay, Paris

Like all the painters of the Impressionist generation, Monet was a painter of joyful celebrations and popular festivities. In his work art goes out into the streets to capture life itself. His brasseries by the Seine, revellers outside country inns, sunny picnic parties and lively dances are all pretexts for a celebration of shared gaiety. In this painting republican joy in all its flamboyant colour is on display at the windows lining the streets. 'I liked the flags,' said Monet. 'On the first national day of celebration on 30 June, I went walking in Rue Montorgueil with the tools of my trade. The street was decked out with flags and packed with crowds. I noticed a balcony, climbed the stairs and asked for permission to paint. It was granted. Then I slipped back down incognito.' In our own times the French day of national celebration is 14 July, but it's still an opportunity for a party.

lines of the flags seem almost alive and fill most of the space, creating a kind of gorge, with the crowds thronging at the bottom. This painting expresses the full force of happiness at its height. It may seem odd to link the words happiness and force, but happiness is a force, and it can change the world.

'ARTICLE 1: THE GOAL OF SOCIETY
IS THE COMMON HAPPINESS.'

DECLARATION OF THE RIGHTS OF MAN AND THE CITIZEN OF 24 JUNE 1793,
KNOWN AS THE 'MONTAGNARD' DECLARATION.

MONET'S LESSON:
HAPPINESS CAN CHANGE THE WORLD

The American Declaration of Independence of 1776 states 'that all men are created equal, that they are endowed by their Creator with certain unalienable Rights, that among these are Life, Liberty and the pursuit of Happiness'. Like post-Revolutionary France, the emerging United States placed great importance, not on happiness, but on the *pursuit* of happiness, which was enshrined in its Declaration of Independence. It is no coincidence to find that the intelligent eighteenth century took an interest in the democratisation of happiness. The politicians of the day had already understood that their role was not to make their fellow citizens happy, but to enable them to attain happiness. Sadly, this lesson was forgotten by the twentieth century with its totalitarian ideologies. For happiness can never be a matter of decree; it always arises out of individual action. But 'individual' is not the same thing as 'selfish' since, unlike sadness and pain, being happy is never about standing still and turning inwards.

In fact happiness is an amazing driver of action.

So what is the origin of the strange but commonplace idea that happiness makes people slow and satisfied and stops them wanting to act? Or the view – so widespread that we unthinkingly accept it despite a vast array of evidence to the contrary – that anxiety is the best spur to reflection and creativity? While anxiety can be a trigger, there is no better motivation over the long term than happiness, or the desire for happiness. This is confirmed by all the studies conducted by psychologists.

Happiness, like all forms of well-being, is an inexhaustible source of the desire to act and the enjoyment of action, of altruism, creativity, receptiveness and curiosity about the world.

Another equally mistaken belief is that happiness makes us soft and mediocre. It is said to immobilise us and make us apathetic. This view may be based on a confusion between serenity and passivity, although the two look alike only from a distance. Perhaps those who accept and perpetuate this belief do so out of their own inability to act unless driven by negative emotions.

It's true that anger and resentment can push us to rebel, react, fight and destroy things that are unjust and unacceptable. But only a desire for and love of happiness, our own and that of others, can help us rebuild afterwards.

'HAPPY BEING. BEING WHAT?
JUST BEING.'

JULIEN GREEN

Happiness can be a revolutionary force. The joyful impulse of the crowds painted by Monet is like that of a river, full of benevolent power, gently making its way into the future. Its movement is reminiscent of the dreams of happiness that lead to great revolutions. For almost all human beings, it is the aspiration to happiness that inspires change and gives it life and strength.

But such dreams are then appropriated by a handful of fanatics, who are always cast from the same mould – frustrated, unhappy and greedy for power because they don't know how to enjoy life. They may sometimes be very learned, but they always lack education in happiness. Once they take power, revolutions tip over into terror until, quietly but inexorably, happiness re-emerges, and the little joys of everyday life are revived.

For, deep down inside human beings, the aspiration to happiness is sovereign. We need to know how to protect and defend it against those who seek to subdue or stifle it.

We must avoid getting sidetracked into hate and bloodletting, which are pointless anyway. For in the end, happiness always wins.

'WHAT HAS NEVER BEEN SAID ENOUGH
IS THAT WE ALSO OWE IT TO OTHERS
TO BE HAPPY.'

ALAIN

WHAT MAKES FOR
HAPPINESS?

Few forms of happiness spring from nowhere. This is what Chagall reminds us in this hymn to the country life showing a Russian peasant in his everyday world, toothless but visibly happy. He is feeding leaves and small flowers to his horse. Around them are scenes from ordinary life, in a joyful whirling spiral. Inside a traditional wooden house painted red, a lamp lights up an animated discussion between two men. Outside we see a tree in the garden, a cart trundling along the road and a joyfully dancing couple. Chagall is offering us a world of simple, everyday happiness, in the

Peasant Life
Marc Chagall (1887–1985)
1925, oil on canvas, 100 x 81 cm,
Albright-Knox Art Gallery, Buffalo.

'No power can terrify me to the point where I lose my faith in human beings. Because I believe in the grandeur of all of nature. I know that human desires and behaviour are often the endpoint of cosmic forces set in motion by nature, by the unfolding of history and the march of destiny.' Throughout his life, Chagall was interested in the political movements of his time, from revolutionary ideals to anti-Semitism, and in the psychological needs of human beings, such as dreams and the quest for happiness.

deluge of colour that was his trademark. 'I am nothing but a man of colours,' he liked to tease.

Chagall was always careful with both his happiness and his independence and here perhaps he gives his answer to the most fundamental question: what do we need to feel happy? Because happiness cannot come out of nowhere. Like everything that has life – and happiness is a living thing – it needs to be nourished. Our immaterial happiness relies on material substance to enable it to come into the world and exist.

'IS THERE ANY HAPPINESS IN THE HOUSE?
SILLY BOY! THERE'S ENOUGH TO BLOW OUT
THE DOORS AND WINDOWS.'

MAURICE MAETERLINCK

Chagall's Lesson:
IN PRAISE OF SIMPLE HAPPINESS

What is the substance of happiness? And how should we view it? Contrary to received ideas, Epicurean philosophy did not advocate that to attain happiness we should give free rein to all our desires and satisfy them. Epicurus did favour a form of hedonism (we are alive in order to feel pleasure), but it was also a form of asceticism, which assumed that we are capable of renouncing empty pleasures and those we can never satisfy.

We need the lucidity to turn towards only those sources of pleasure that Epicurus calls 'natural and necessary', such as food, a roof over our heads and clothing, and also freedom, friends and discussion, reflective thought (I daren't say *philosophy*, but that was what Epicurus was really advocating). None of the rest – power, money, glory – is indispensable.

We don't need to make huge efforts not to pursue superfluous things that might offer happiness. The important thing is not to allow ourselves to become fooled by or dependent on them.

'YOU SEE THAT THERE ARE FEW PRINCIPLES
TO MASTER IN ORDER TO LEAD A HAPPY
AND PIOUS LIFE. IF YOU RESPECT THESE, THE GODS
WILL ASK NOTHING MORE FROM YOU.'

MARCUS AURELIUS

No search for happiness can be understood out of the context of its period. When the historians of eudaemonism – the philosophy of happiness – consider the period of the twentieth and twenty-first centuries, they will doubtless be surprised to discover just how much the consumer society desired happiness, and used its pursuit to sell pointless things.

They will wonder how this acquisitiveness captured the attention of the most vulnerable among us – and in reality all of us at different times and to differing degrees – to the point where we gave up trying to understand what happiness is made of and focused instead on buying objects to make us happy, with increasingly temporary effects. They will wonder why our societies took so long to react and to teach their citizens and children about these traps, so that they could better protect themselves from falling into them. But that's another story ...

Here's an exercise in discernment: ask yourself, what do I really need in order to be happy? And what are others trying to persuade me that I need?

Through his portrait of peasant life, Chagall reminds us that happiness cannot be reduced to a simple state of mind or decision. It requires the presence of a basic minimum of relationships and material elements. Below a certain threshold of loneliness and material vulnerability, we can think only of how to survive. If we are hungry, cold, lonely and afraid for our very lives, we cannot begin to think of happiness. The best we can hope for in such situations is a break from our misfortune and sufferings – relief rather than happiness. So, for most people on the planet, happiness is first of all having shelter and enough to eat, and being able to live, think and speak freely. It's only because these fundamental needs have been satisfied for most of us Westerners living in democracies that we can start trying to make ourselves happier.

However elementary and simple they may be, these fundamental requirements for happiness are still indispensable. Let's rejoice that we have them every day.

'WE CAN SETTLE FOR A LITTLE COARSE RICE AND A LITTLE WATER TO LIVE ON, A BENT ARM FOR A PILLOW, AND STILL FIND HAPPINESS. RICHES AND HONOUR ARE NO MORE TO ME THAN PASSING CLOUDS.'

CONFUCIUS

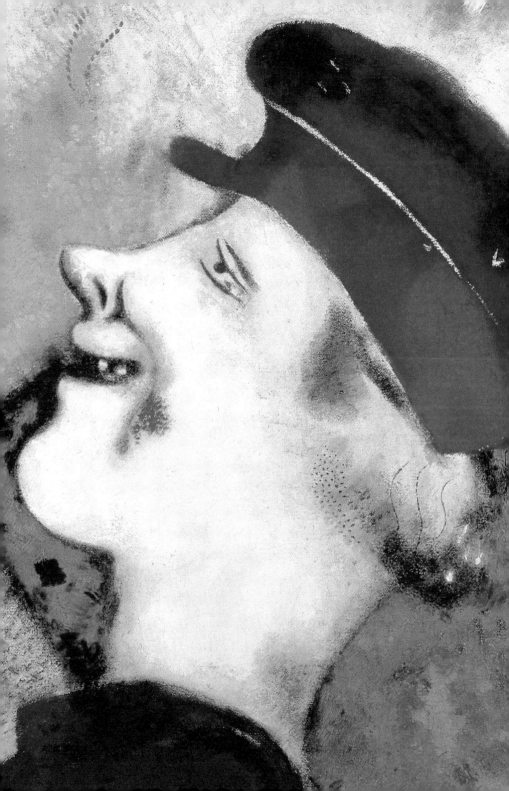

THE
INTELLIGENCE
OF HAPPINESS

s happiness a state of mind? Is it a mental operation? A decision? An effort? An act of will? An inner construction? It tends to be all these things, once the basic material conditions necessary for its presence are in place. This is both good news – our happiness depends on us – and bad news – so we are responsible for it. It requires us to put in some work and effort.

Figure on a Blue Background
Gaston Chaissac (1910–1964)
1959, oil on board, 66 x 44.7 cm
Musée des Beaux-Arts, Nantes.

Gaston Chaissac was born into a poor family, which his father soon abandoned. He started out as a kitchen boy, before becoming a shoe-maker in Paris, where he lived with his brother, a policeman. Their neighbours were a couple of artists who encouraged Chaissac to take up painting. His talent was recognised in the artistic circles of the day, notably by Dubuffet. But Chaissac moved to the Vendée region in western France and pursued his artistic work with little by way of income other than his wife's salary as a primary school teacher. Judging from his letters, happiness did not come easily to him. So from where did the radiant smiles that appear throughout his work get their warmth and hope?

This apparently tormented figure, with a body that's barely drawn at all, no arms and legs and an unattractive yet radiantly smiling face, is a kind of mischievous mirror that the artist, Gaston Chaissac, holds up to himself. This sickly, melancholic painter reminds us that happiness is never – or very seldom – a gift. However, it's always accessible to the mighty power of human intelligence. With a big smile full of strength and generous confidence, and mocking eyes that are also attentive, wondering and – crucially – wide open to the world, this figure makes me think of my friend Alexandre Jollien, a philosopher with a damaged body and champion of the 'joyful fight' for a thoughtfully happy life. This painting also reminds us of the most important thing, which is that happiness has its own intelligence. Some have a talent for it, others struggle, but it is accessible to us all.

CHAISSAC'S LESSON:
WORK ON YOUR HAPPINESS

What is the source of that strange received idea that happiness has to be spontaneous and that striving to achieve it is not productive and may even be counter-productive? Why so many criticisms of the pursuit of happiness? Be they self-aggrandising poses of pseudo-realism or sincerely held beliefs, all these ideas are rooted in our Biblical heritage. From this we learn that, before original sin, Adam and Eve lived a naturally happy life in the Garden of Eden. This natural state was then taken from them by the wrath of God and can't be regained through our own efforts. It can be granted to us only through divine grace.

The same well-worn idea has another source in the fantasy of the pure happiness of childhood. According to this, the fact that we were so good at being happy when we were children, effortlessly and unawares, means we should be able to return to this original state without having to work for it, simply by digging deep enough into ourselves, or breaking down certain barriers. This is the myth of the return to the source, which operates in some forms of psychotherapy.

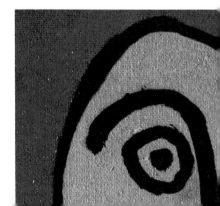

Such ideas are not always entirely wrong. But neither are they enough. The divine punishment handed down to our ancestors Adam and Eve, 'You will earn your bread by the sweat of your brow', also signified, 'You will earn part of your happiness by the sweat of your brow', regardless of whether the cause was divine anger or the human condition.

Happiness is about intelligence rather than luck. It can be learned and developed.

It's often said that life is a struggle. Well so is happiness, particularly for those who were not born into good fortune. Whether our handicaps are visible, such as disabilities that affect our bodies, or invisible, such as those rooted in our past, our anxieties or our tendency to melancholy, they always give us many reasons not to be happy. But once we have established the eternal truth that some people are happier than us and others are less happy, what excuse is there for continuing to ruminate on our wretchedness? Seeing ourselves as life's victims is all the more dangerous because it can turn us into untouchables whom no one wants to approach, guide or advise. This makes our loneliness and difficulties more acute and will ultimately make us shrink into ourselves.

We alone can fight our way to greater emotional light; we alone can prefer happiness to misery.

We can make a decision to be happy, though there's no guarantee of immediate success. Obviously it's more than just a matter of saying, 'Today I'm going to be happy.' We need to say, 'I'm going to spend time and energy thinking and acting in a way that will increase my chances of feeling happy as often as possible. It's not about being happy just like that, here and now, whistling up happiness like a dog. But I can pave the way for happiness. I can open my eyes and my mind, in the same way that I make myself present when I'm walking in a forest, instead of remaining wrapped in my worries about yesterday and tomorrow.' We can't always be ready to make this effort and to take this path. In fact some days it's impossible. At these times we cannot bear talk of happiness – we're not open to it. And yet the decision to be happy also applies to the dark days. At these times I sink no further than necessary; I don't allow my sadness, however justified, to undermine everything.

We can't always be happy. But we can remember to leave the way open for happiness to return.

'INTO THE FRAY! I MUST TAKE ADVANTAGE
OF LIFE AND FIND JOY OR I AM LOST.
BUT HOW AM I GOING TO DO IT?'

ALEXANDRE JOLLIEN

THE BREATH OF
LOVE

A couple sit with their backs to us. The man and woman are holding hands, indifferent to our watching eyes. They are looking at the approaching shoreline and its tall buildings. Is this a place they are seeing for the first time, or are they returning home? Is this the end of a lovely day out, or a long and difficult sea crossing?

We will never know the answers to these questions, we can only imagine them. As always in Friedrich's work, the painting arouses the viewer's curiosity and makes us

On the Sailing Boat
Caspar David Friedrich (1774–1840)
1818–1820, oil on canvas, 71 x 56 cm,
Hermitage Museum, St Petersburg.

On 21 January 1818 Caspar Friedrich married Caroline Bommer. For their honeymoon he took his young wife to the shores of the Baltic and the island of Rügen. Shortly after his return to Dresden, he portrayed himself in this light-filled painting, seen from behind with Caroline. It's a simple, beautiful depiction of love, in which Friedrich has avoided all tired – and limiting – images of a kiss or embrace.

engage with its suggested mystery. The painter is also asking us to think about what it is to be a couple and the nature of love.

The entire foreground is plunged in shadow. The captain steering the ship is outside the picture, in exactly the place where we stand to look at it. The sky above the couple looks threatening. Only the city in the distance is bathed in a light that could be of either dawn or dusk.

Rather than simply portraying two young people in love, Friedrich has subtly evoked the obscure forces that impel a couple towards their destiny, the areas of darkness and light that surround them and the mystery of their future. At the heart of all this is the love that binds them, and on which their future life together depends.

'YOU WILL BE LOVED WHEN YOU CAN SHOW YOUR WEAKNESS WITHOUT THE OTHER USING IT TO ASSERT THEIR OWN STRENGTH.'

CESARE PAVESE

FRIEDRICH'S LESSON:
WHAT MAKES A
COUPLE HAPPY

Is love indispensable to happiness? Almost certainly, but not at any price, or under any conditions.

The Ancients were wary of passionate love. They saw it as a dangerous state of blindness and insanity. The Romantics, on the other hand, made it the cornerstone of their worldview. The intense happiness we feel as love emerges, and particularly if it is shared, is totally fulfilling, freeing us from everything else around us and removing all our material needs (as reflected in the phrase 'to live on love alone'). Love makes us light-hearted and benevolent. It makes us see life as finer than it is.

This state is precious because it makes happiness tangible and it can make us feel fulfilled. *Totally.* Of course the future will reveal that this feeling cannot last, but in the moment we believe it will. We can't imagine how it could come to an end. This experience of happiness, which is infinitely intense though it will not last for ever, is crucial. But it is a state of joy that has to come to an end. It's a prelude to other forms of happiness and a kind of intoxication that shows us that the world can change if something inside us changes. The chemistry at work here isn't due to alcohol, but love. It's like an illumination, a deluge of happiness. Aside from the great mystics, few people have such experiences of pure, intense happiness in their lives.

Passionate love gives us an experience of total happiness. This in itself is wonderful and exceptional.

But love is not enough. This observation marks the first disillusionment of life as a couple. Loving each other is not enough in itself to make us happy together, or make us happier together than we might be alone. Other conditions and – as always where happiness is concerned – other efforts are required. These could be summed up in the motto: 'Liberty, equality, fraternity', because what is true of republican society is also true of the primary society that is the couple.

Let's start with liberty. It is not so easy to grant the other person the freedom of their own thoughts (letting them keep their secrets, not wanting to know everything about them, their past and present), feelings (accepting that their love has its doubts) and movement (absence and distance can make the heart grow fonder, and allows each lover to breathe). Then let's take equality, which involves noticing and maintaining a long-term balance in the matter of chores and obligations, because small imbalances can lead to big frustrations that make life as a couple seem more of a hindrance than an aid to happiness. Lastly, fraternity means nurturing my partner's happiness in a sincere, altruistic way, even if this means I must rein in my own, or accept certain constraints, at least for now. Friedrich proposes another source of conjugal happiness in the form of joint action. This can also ward off Nietzsche's prediction that 'Love can only be a pitiful well-being for two, a long idiocy'.

Love does not express itself solely through the fusion of two people, but also in shared action and construction, in making a way through life together.

The philosophers tell us that love is not all about passion. In fact, it takes three forms: *Eros*, *Philia* and *Agape*.

Eros is love born of desire and a sense of lack. It is passionate, possessive love. It's a source of great happiness when reciprocated, of great suffering when it is not. *Eros* is love as it first emerges and its natural destiny is to die. Our minds and bodies couldn't cope with chronic passionate love for years at a stretch. But in the best-case scenario it can regularly rekindle from its ashes, either for the same person – which is a happy thing for a couple – or for someone else, with more difficult consequences. It produces immense, intense happiness, which theorists tend to call joy.

However, there are other forms of love, nourished less by the body and more by the mind, or even the soul. *Philia* is love that's akin to friendship. For a couple it doesn't have to be a secondary, worn and weary form of love. It's something else. There are loving friendships and friendships between lovers. These provide just as much happiness as passionate love – if not more. They certainly generate less unhappiness. *Philia* is a love that can allow its object to be somewhere else and have room to breathe, without suffering the pain of absence and distance. This love wants happiness for the other person, not just for itself by being with them all the time. It can be found in couples who have been together for a while, but we also see it in the love of parents for their children. And of course, it is present in friendship, that reciprocal form of affection, esteem and sharing.

Agape is the most altruistic form of love. It makes us able to feel love for people who are not close to us, and even for people we don't know. Can we love all human beings? Obviously this makes *Agape* the most difficult of the three forms of love, because it's the most foreign to our habits, reflexes and needs. We're more inclined to love those we know, when we should also learn to know those we love. This is *charity*, the neighbourly love of the Christian tradition. It's perhaps more the fruit of a philosophical attitude than an instinct or psychological aptitude.

While emerging happiness such as love may initially stem from a kind of selfishness (looking after ourselves) – though it may be tempered and respectful of others – we shall see that over the longer term happiness can only be fulfilled through an ever deeper, stronger connection to our surroundings.

We need to leave *Eros* behind and move towards *Philia*, and then *Agape*. This is the lesson that takes us from love to happiness in concentric circles, as we gradually move away from ourselves and open up in order to give.

ONLY
CONNECT

A father and his young son stand facing the painter. Both are dressed in dark colours, allowing our attention to focus on the beauty of their faces and the ermine on the little boy's coat. The father's expression is strong and calm. He looks out towards the viewer and his

Iseppo da Ponto and his Son Adriano
Paolo Caliari, known as Veronese
(1528–1588)
1555, oil on canvas, 247 x 137cm, Palazzo Pitti, Florence.

'Simple in his deeds, faithful to his promises, he always preserved the dignity of his person and profession. He had none of the violent passions, resounding hatreds or pride-fuelled quarrels that tarnished the glory of some of that period's great geniuses. The exercise of his art and the education of his children, which he conducted himself with extreme care, were enough to fill his whole life.' This is the portrait of Veronese offered by his biographer Ridolfi.

It seems that Paolo Caliari, known as Veronese, was what is called a happy man. A stonecutter's son, he left his native Verona for Venice, the magnificent city governed by the Doges, who soon gave him both recognition and many commissions. He married a woman he loved, the daughter of his master Antonio Badile, he had many children and friends and enjoyed unblemished success. Veronese's painting reflects the joy, certainty and serenity of his life. His style portrays the richness and magnificence of Renaissance Venice. This portrait reveals a more personal, intimate side of Veronese. The artist, whose own sons Gabriele and Carletto became his main collaborators, has almost certainly put something of himself into this depiction of the paternal bond.

features are relaxed, but we can see the gleaming leather of his gloved hand resting on his sword.

The son's thoughts are elsewhere. Weary of posing, he looks away, playing with the hand that his father has placed on his shoulder in a gesture of affection mixed with authority. This painting is all about the son's hands on the father's hand. And to me it is one of the finest paintings about connection. This combination of affectionate anchoring, caresses and play expresses all the force and complexity of the bond between not only father and son, but all human beings. The father is there as a guide, model and protector. The child moves his father's hand on his shoulder, he plays with it, feels it without looking. His father's presence and love will enable the son to face the world one day, and to live in it happily.

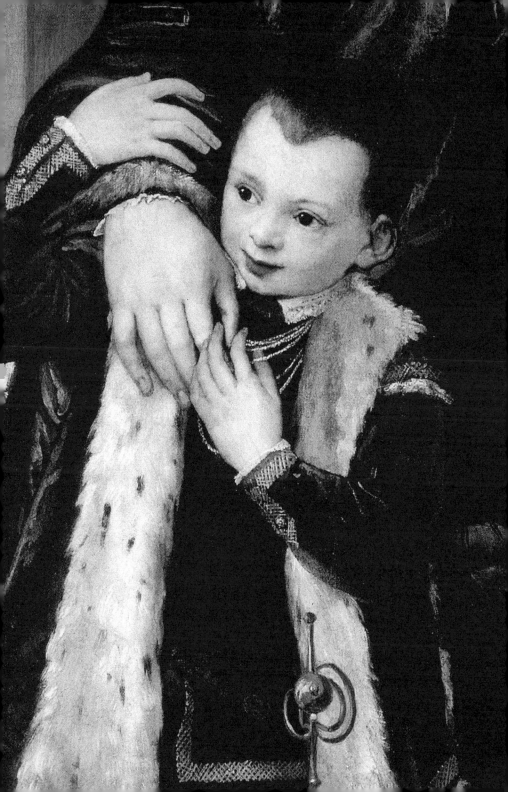

VERONESE'S LESSON:
AFFECTION AND GRATITUDE NURTURE HAPPINESS

Happiness circulates between people. We receive it, we pass it on, and every time it passes from one person to the next it regenerates, transforms itself, changes, acquires meaning and a history. As with life itself, we are simply its vessels and transmitters.

Affection – that form of love that doesn't seek to possess and accepts others for what they are, which wants the best for them – fosters happiness. For it's a love that gives more than it asks in return, which is more about releasing than clasping, and rejoices in the happiness of its object. Of course some relationships can be alienating. Love can be possessive and stifling and so, sometimes, can friendship. This is why some people are suspicious of any form of attachment, which they regard as too often associated with an infinite potential for pain, such as the pain of being abandoned, of seeing those we love suffer, or of not being loved in return.

But the only way to free ourselves from this fear of love, this anxiety that we will not receive enough in return, is to give – to love altruistically, through the altruistic parental love Veronese shows us here, or through friendly affection.

Love works in virtuous circles. One of these is gratitude. I can be grateful to many people for the happiness they have given me. Science teaches us that this gratitude will in turn increase our happiness. Hence the strange 'gratitude exercises' that psychotherapists prescribe for their patients. Doctors do this too, because gratitude has beneficial effects for health. A grateful heart acquires *cardiac coherence* – it beats more slowly and more regularly. The brain too seems to benefit from these waves of gratitude, as shown by studies using digital imaging. Psychological research seems to show that things given to us by others tend to bring us more happiness than the things we have acquired for ourselves.

Fortunately, there's no lack of opportunities for gratitude. Like happiness, they just require us to make a little effort to open up, focus and think – for example about all the people who have helped us become who we are, such as parents, grandparents, other relations, friends and teachers. All the people who have shared moments in our lives and have brought us happiness or shown us how to get closer to it, through their love, affection and attention. We can also feel gratitude to strangers, for a smile or a helping hand, a mark of

'BETWEEN US THERE IS SOMETHING
MORE THAN LOVE – COMPLICITY.'
MARGUERITE YOURCENAR

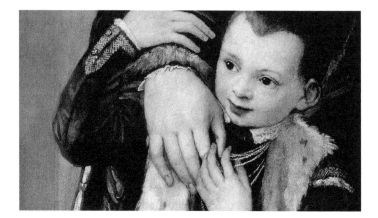

respect, an act of kindness or simply for being polite. Realising how much our happiness owes to others makes us happy in itself and offers us happy memories.

Happiness is never hurt by feeling indebted to others. In fact it's more likely to suffer from a failure to recognise and accept this debt. It grows when it is nourished with gratitude, the 'happy feeling of a boundless debt', as the philosopher Vladimir Jankélévitch puts it.

It's said that the music of Bach was painful to the philosopher Cioran – it was too beautiful, too perfect, too divine. In her fine essay on the 'teachers of despair', Nancy Houston observes this strange view of existence with surprise. If Bach's music makes us cry, it's with tears of joy! And of gratitude too for the extraordinary human chain that links Bach not only to instrument makers and musicians, but also to the engineers whose work produced the recordings and devices that enable us to listen to music when there are no musicians present, the factory workers who made these devices and many, many others besides.

This more or less universal gratitude is possible only with a minimum of humility. We have to recognise how much our happiness owes to others. But this humility also makes us able to receive many other forms of happiness, such as feeling that we are the heirs to all of human intelligence and the altruism of those who have thought, built and acted before us and, ultimately, for us.

I like the amazement we feel when we make the emotional (and not just intellectual) discovery that it isn't necessary to know people to feel gratitude towards them. We feel a dizzy rush of joy as our feeling of gratitude expands to include the entire human race – and therefore to Veronese, who gave us this painting and the emotion and thoughts it awakens within us. Théophile Gautier wrote: 'No painter had a greater, higher ideal. The eternal celebration of his paintings has a deeper meaning. It constantly shows human beings the real goal, the ideal that never deceives, happiness, which unintelligent moralists want to relegate to the other world. […] So all glory to Paul Veronese, who sets gleaming before our eyes the elements of happiness that divine benevolence has put at our disposal!'

HAPPINESS BEYOND
OURSELVES

'Blessed Francis met a poorly dressed nobleman who had fallen on hard times and, moved to affectionate pity by the man's destitution, took off his own mantle and gave it to him.'

Jacques de Voragine, *La Légende dorée.*

In this magnificent fresco, Giotto shows St Francis of Assisi in his youth. Shortly after this episode of the gift of his mantle, Francis, the son of a rich city merchant, gave up all his property, right down to his clothes, to devote himself to the poor. He gained the nickname *il poverello*, 'the little poor man'. Francis had understood where his own happiness lay. He could see how to become extremely happy and his first concern was not only to shed all that he regarded as an obstacle to his chosen form of happiness (his vow of poverty), but also to share this happiness through the gift of a coat, a smile and an example.

Happiness cannot live, breathe and grow unless it is shared and passed on. As a wise man said one day, 'What you give, you gain. What you keep, you lose.'

The Gift of the Mantle
Giotto di Bondone (1266–1337)
*1297–1299, wall painting, 270 x 225 cm,
Upper Church, Assisi.*

On the tomb of St Francis of Assisi a church was built that became the fourth most important pilgrimage destination in mediaeval Christendom, after Jerusalem, Rome and Compostela. In a cycle of twenty-eight wall paintings, completed between 1297 and 1299, Giotto and his pupils depicted the main episodes of the life of Saint Francis and the miracles worked after his death, making this the most decorated basilica in all of Europe. *The Gift of the Mantle* is one of the finest frescos in the cycle. It was almost certainly the first to be painted and, according to the experts, most of it is the work of Giotto himself. The painter's life seems to have been a long way from the ideal of poverty advocated by Saint Francis and the Franciscan order that he founded. Giotto was regarded as a national hero in Florence, the equal of Dante – who was almost certainly his friend – and he was not indifferent to honours. However, while he may not have been the painter of the poor, like Saint Francis, Giotto had a vision of the world in which human beings and profane things have a dignity and radiance that had previously been reserved for holy figures.

Giotto's Lesson:
SHARING AND GIVING ARE THE DUTIES OF HAPPY PEOPLE

'If you're happy, you're in the wrong', wrote Philippe Delerm. Can happiness be an offence against the misery of the world? Can it hurt those who are not or are no longer happy, or who don't manage to be happy? Why this prejudice? Perhaps it's because happiness is a form of wealth – no doubt the greatest and most important of all, the one that absorbs and replaces all the others, rendering them pointless and empty. Perhaps it's because all forms of wealth hurt those who are poor. And there are people who are poor in happiness. But then what are the origins of that other, equally strange and false, belief that the happiness of some diminishes, or can diminish, the happiness of others? Perhaps it arises when happiness is confused with pride in happiness. Hence the cliché – so often disproved by scientific research – that happiness is 'selfish'. In fact we know that, far from making people more selfish, happiness leads to an increase in acts of altruism. Perhaps ultimately these prejudices stem from an allergy to happiness on the part of those who find it hard to be happy.

Happiness is a form of wealth, not a sin. So it should not be condemned or punished, but of course it does impose duties of modesty and generosity.

Happiness expands the boundaries of the self and so naturally reinforces our feelings of fraternity with our fellows – no doubt because it increases both our empathy and our awareness of the fragility of living beings. This is why the act of individual realisation that accompanies the emergence of happiness ('my happiness depends on me and my struggles') can – must? – be transformed into an act of political awareness ('the happiness of others too depends on me and my struggles'). Martin Luther King, recalling Marcus Aurelius, observed that the violence done to human beings is not only the result of the actions of bad people, but also of the inaction of good people.

Happiness is a driver of change in the world, not because it gets talked about, but because it enables altruistic action.

Happiness slowly fades, losing colour and vigour, when it grows only in the soils of the ego. Hence its tendency to circulate and be passed on, and the fact that, ultimately, it's more contagious than we think. We all prefer the company of happy people, as long as they're happy in a sober way, not proud of their happiness or intoxicated by it. Sometimes the passing

'THE AIM IS TO BE HAPPY. WE GET THERE ONLY SLOWLY, IT TAKES DAILY APPLICATION. ONCE WE ARE HAPPY THERE'S STILL A LOT TO DO – WE MUST COMFORT OTHERS.'

JULES RENARD

of happiness from one person to another slows down and seizes up under the weight of too many worries, fears, moments of indifference and small, casual acts of selfishness. When this happens it must be restarted, awakened from its drowsiness, and this is brought about by tiny deeds – a gift, a smile, a kindness – that are also marks of social decency in relation to our fellow human beings. The awareness that transforms well-being into happiness gives it an added meaning that is political and ecological.

For there is also an ecology of happiness that involves maintaining an environment that allows it to blossom, and this is a political act. Gide said, 'Never accept any form of happiness that is obtained to the detriment of the greatest number.' Does this concern for others make our well-being and comfort more fragile and complicated? Possibly. But it also expands and reinforces our happiness.

There's no pettiness or retraction in happiness, just the expansion of our consciousness towards ever greater humanity.

'TODAY WHEN MY LIFE, SAFETY, FREEDOM
AND HAPPINESS DEPEND ON THE SUPPORT
OF MY FELLOWS, IT IS CLEAR THAT I SHOULD
NO LONGER REGARD MYSELF AS AN INDIVIDUAL,
ISOLATED BEING, BUT AS PART OF A GREAT WHOLE.'

JEAN-JACQUES ROUSSEAU

EVENING
THE TWILIGHTS
OF HAPPINESS

THE MELANCHOLY OF HAPPINESS ENDING
Watteau, Pilgrimage to the Island of Cythera

EVERY HAPPINESS HAS AN ELEMENT
OF DARKNESS
Sargent, Ena and Betty, Daughters of Asher and Mrs Wertheimer

THE TEMPTATION OF SORROW
Gauguin, Faaturuma

ENTERING THE WINTER OF HAPPINESS
Bruegel, The Return of the Herd

THE
MELANCHOLY
OF HAPPINESS ENDING

Sadly, we must go. It was a wonderful party, but it's coming to an end. A joyful, busy group are joining the path while others walk calmly down the hill. The bust of Venus will soon be alone again in the shadow of the trees, its plinth garlanded with roses in memory of the happy time spent here. Clouds are beginning to darken the sky. The day is almost over.

See how the three couples on the right of the picture hold the viewer's attention. Each illustrates a moment or a way of reacting to the subtle pain of happiness ending. On the far right a man tries to use these last moments to seduce his companion. In a ridiculous, touching act of denial, he's trying to ignore the fact that it's time to go. The second couple are taking it all very calmly, the man helping his companion to her feet. Both seem to accept the obvious fact that this is the end and it's time to go home. Meanwhile, the man in the couple on the left is seen from behind – his mind is already elsewhere – while the woman glances back one last time with a sad smile. Is she trying to soak up everything she has just experienced, not realising that other, similar moments will come her way?

What should we do with our happiness as it declines? Should we cling feverishly to it? Weep for its loss in advance? Isn't it better to accept its end with serenity?

Pilgrimage to the Island of Cythera

Antoine Watteau (1684–1721)
1717, oil on canvas, 128 x 193 cm
Musée du Louvre, Paris.

Watteau painted this picture in the evening of his short life, before dying of tuberculosis. He was without family, fortune or a home, but he did have friends who cared for him in his last moments. Though his work was appreciated by a small circle of admirers, Watteau was never regarded as an official painter. His life in no way resembled the subjects he painted. We might imagine him as a pleasure-loving socialite, but in fact he was shy and bad-tempered. It's easy to infer that he must always have viewed happiness with a mixture of anticipation and pain – every moment contains within it the certainty of its end – which might explain the indescribable sense of nostalgia that pervades his paintings, even when they portray festivities and happy moments. It was said that he was the painter of subtle emotions, not yet conscious to those who feel them. In this departure from Cythera – the mythical isle to which Aphrodite was carefully transported by the Zephyrs after her birth from the foam – Watteau conveys this sense of the decline of happiness and the gentle sadness that goes with it.

'WHEN THE CALL OF HAPPINESS IS TOO MUCH, SADNESS CAN ARISE IN HUMAN HEARTS.'

ALBERT CAMUS

WATTEAU'S LESSON: EMBRACE DECLINE, EVEN THAT OF HAPPINESS

Things that we have loved and are about to disappear take on a sudden beauty and grace. Something we see for the last time acquires a strange charm, like the volatile pain of a leave-taking that we sense will be our last farewell to a happy moment.

What Watteau seems to be saying is that anyone who has not felt this pain in their heart has never known happiness. It is perhaps in moments such as these, he suggests, that the very essence of happiness lies. A cloud passes before the sun, conversations stall, eyes are suddenly veiled by sadness – in such moments the festive mood changes. A tiny detail breaks the spell and makes us feel that these moments have been merely a parenthesis. Such subtle moments, like Watteau's painting, combine pleasure (it was so wonderful), melancholy (how sad that we must part) and worry (what now?).

We're all painfully sensitive to these moments when happiness fades. It's pointless to struggle against the tide, forcing laughter and pretending nothing is happening. Far better to let go with a gentle smile. The decline of happiness is still happiness.

'BEWARE THE SWEETNESS OF THINGS,
WHEN YOUR HEART FEELS TOO HEAVY
AND BEATS FOR NO REASON.'

PAUL-JEAN TOULET

This intangible, inevitable dissolution of happiness is very mysterious. When I was a child I read about that scatterbrained genius Leonardo da Vinci, who decided one day to test a new fixative he had invented on one of his frescos. Unfortunately, it turned out that the new substance was highly corrosive and the painter realised that the fresco on which he had worked so patiently was about to be destroyed. I remember wondering how he reacted. At the moment when he realised that his fresco was doomed, did he fly into a great rage, or sink into despair? Today I imagine Leonardo sighing, then smiling, sitting down and mustering all the strength and focus at his command to watch the fleeting, magnificent sight of his fresco disappearing for ever, preferring one last happiness to pointless, empty fury. The idea that all happiness is doomed to vanish is certainly painful. But once the countdown has begun, what can we do?

We can only learn to admire and love happiness ending. We must understand its coming and going as the endless, immense and rhythmic breath of our earthly happiness.

'I KNOW I SHALL NEVER BE HAPPIER THAN NOW.
I SPEAK THE NAME OF MY HAPPINESS;
SUDDENLY IT FRIGHTENS ME
AND GIVES ME GOOSE-BUMPS.'

PHILIPPE DELERM

EVERY HAPPINESS HAS AN
ELEMENT OF DARKNESS

I n the period known as the Belle Époque a world was about to disappear, but didn't yet know it. On view today at the Tate Britain, London, Sargent's painting immediately draws our attention with its imposing size. Visitors first admire the delicate beauty of Betty, the younger of the two sisters, in her elegant red velvet gown. Then their eyes are drawn to the radiant vitality of her elder sister Ena, the painter's favourite, in her gown of white satin. Everything about her speaks of life's happiness, from her high colour to her

Ena and Betty, Daughters of Asher and Mrs Wertheimer
John Singer Sargent (1856–1925)
1901, oil on canvas, 185 x 130 cm, Tate Gallery, London.

American artist John Singer Sargent was a cosmopolitan figure. Born in Florence, he spent his working life in Europe and died in London. He is regarded as one

of his period's most brilliant painters of high-society portraits and was very close to the Wertheimer family, painting all its members. Before his death Sargent was witness to the end of Belle Époque and the collapse of its carefree, happy society into the horrors of the First World War, which he depicted in many paintings.

proudly raised head, smile and impatient gesture. Although her left hand rests nonchalantly on a magnificent Chinese vase – owned by her father, a very rich art dealer – with her other arm Ena seems to want to lead her sister away.

However, gradually, the viewer is overcome by a strange melancholy. Where does it spring from? Is it the darkness and bourgeois comfort we glimpse in the background, redolent of the leaden atmosphere of a Victorian interior? Or is it a sadness linked to the romantic idea that these young women bursting with life are now dust and ashes, along with the world they embodied? Or is it simply that any depiction of happiness arouses the same feelings when we look at it carefully. 'Things of beauty are those that cause us despair,' said Paul Valéry, and perhaps the same is true of happiness.

SARGENT'S LESSON:
DO NOT FEAR THE SUBTLE PAIN OF HAPPINESS

Summer has barely started and already the days are getting shorter. At their height all moments of happiness can cause us sadness. We sometimes find it hard to accept the obvious fact that happiness can make us unhappy. We are calm, serene and satisfied. The surface of our life is as smooth as the sea before the breeze picks up and there are no clouds on our horizon. And yet, we feel overcome with an insidious, inexplicable sense of melancholy. Can happiness secrete its own antidote and self-destruct once it reaches a certain point of intensity? The clear awareness of happiness contains the seed of its impending end. We shouldn't see this as an unlikely form of masochism, as though we couldn't bear to be too well, or even as a dubious form of guilt that makes us experience happiness as an offence against or betrayal of the sufferings of others, be they close to us or people we don't know. No, this inner scenario is all about *consciousness*.

Consciousness is necessary to our happiness. It turns animal well-being into the very human feeling of happiness. But once undermined, this same consciousness opens our eyes to the passing, fleeting nature of all happiness.

Our relationship with happiness is intermittent. We are condemned to experience it only through appearance alternating with disappearance, flux and reflux. This means that happiness only seems infinite to us as it emerges – at the point where we begin to feel happy, we don't think about the end of happiness. Everything in our lives that is beginning seems boundless to us, and this boundlessness makes us light-hearted and even more happy. Conversely, things that are coming to an end confine us, they cut us off and make us sad, sometimes unreasonably so, beyond what might be expected. We feel that these small moments of grief for happy times are simply a rehearsal for our own end. So our consciousness, which enables us to achieve the emotional plenitude of happiness, then becomes the vector of our sadness. It reveals the perishable nature of our joys along with everything else, and gives us the intuition that they will soon vanish.

We can't be happy without consciousness. Being aware that we are happy enables our happiness to increase, but it also means accepting that it will be fleeting.

Sometimes we are sad at the thought that our happiness will end after it has been so powerful. In order to avoid the pain of the moment when it disappears, some people try to avoid happiness. It's as though, for them, the temptation to be happy is a guilty, dangerous weakness that will be punished by greater suffering once the illusion has faded.

This attitude often stems from vulnerability. Unable to cope with feeling abandoned by happiness, some people don't allow themselves to feel it at all. But when we try to protect our fragility like this, it can dry us up or lead us to put on an armour of distrust, pessimism, cynicism and an ironic attitude to others – those naïve, credulous, thoughtless fools who give way to a happiness that will sooner or later come to an end.

Conversely, others who are equally fragile but bolder, throw themselves into a perpetual dash for happiness, a feverish pursuit of pleasure. For these people each form of happiness is constantly superseded by the next and the main aim is to leave no gaps between them. Quality is replaced by quantity. 'Pleasure is the only thing one should live for. Nothing ages like happiness', as Oscar Wilde famously said. In my view the phrase would be more true the other way round. But Wilde was a homosexual living in a Victorian society that was particularly sexually repressive (he was sent to prison) and forbade him to be openly happy, leaving him only the consolation of clandestine pleasures.

Faced with the fleeting, intermittent nature of happiness, our recourse to aversion or obsession, those two forms of fear, reflects how hard it is for us

'THOSE WHO SPEAK OF HAPPINESS
OFTEN HAVE SAD EYES.'

LOUIS ARAGON

to accept that our emotional life cannot be stabilised and regulated at will. Some prefer to take permanent refuge in gloom and regard all efforts to arouse or accept happiness with suspicion, maintaining a low but stable state. Others try to remain on a permanent high through constant doses of pleasure. Both approaches lead to denial and weariness, and they are such a waste, since there are so many more fruitful battles to be fought.

Accepting happiness also means learning to accept the pain of its disappearance.

There are two good reasons to accept the un-breakable link between happiness and the anticipated sadness of its dissolution. One is grounded in bio-logical fact: happiness has an emotional basis, and all emotions are by nature perishable. Just as the sun sets

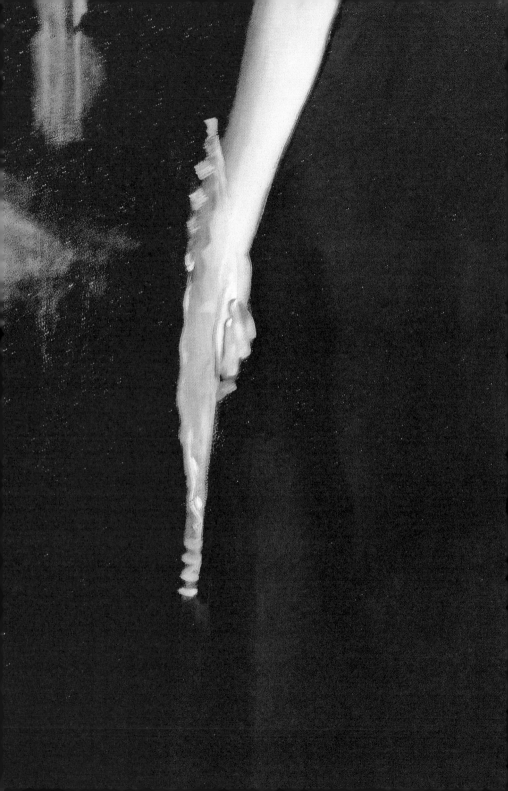

and people go to sleep, so happiness fades. The other reason is that moments of sadness are almost certainly useful. It's impossible to be happy if you bury your head in the sand. Through its dark side happiness reveals that it is rooted in life, which is often sad, and marked by endings, deaths, disappearance, goodbyes and farewells of all kinds and degrees. The role of happiness is not to mask this reality from us, but to give us the strength to face it, and also to bring meaning and light to our lives. We intuitively know that each time our happiness disappears this is a little rehearsal of our own disappearance from the Earth.

No life of lasting happiness is possible without a consideration of death. Happiness is a subtle feeling. It casts its own shadows, which speak to us of life and death. These are things we must accept. This element of darkness gives the light of happiness its full value.

'AND YOU, MY HEART, WHY DO YOU BEAT
LIKE A MELANCHOLY WATCHMAN
I OBSERVE NIGHT AND DEATH'
GUILLAUME APOLLINAIRE

THE TEMPTATION
OF SORROW

The young woman gently rocks in her chair. Our eye is drawn first by the diagonal mass of her dress of magnificent red, then to the melancholy of her face with her absent gaze. Then we notice the white handkerchief held absently in her left hand. Has she been crying? Last of all, we see the rocking chair, which recalls the words of Schopenhauer, the philosopher of unhappiness: 'Life swings like a pendulum backwards and forwards between pain and boredom.'

Faaturuma (Woman in a Red Dress, or Melancholic)
Paul Gauguin (1848–1903)
*1893, oil on canvas, 94 x 68 cm,
Nelson-Atkins Museum of Art, Kansas City.*

Gauguin painted this picture in his first Tahitian period. He had gone in search of an untainted paradise in the islands of Oceania and strove to convince himself that he had found it. But if this painting is to be believed, things were not so simple. One of his biographers speaks of a 'sobering experience of reality', as reflected in the melancholic pose of this young woman in her uncustomary Western dress, no doubt imposed by the missionaries.

This woman who has given in to sorrow is perhaps painted in the image of Gauguin himself, suffering the disillusionment of his first period in Tahiti. He thought to discover a natural paradise there, but found only a vanishing world and the seductive traces of a way of life that was fast disappearing. Faaturuma, this beautiful, brooding woman, seems turned in on herself and absent to the world. This is how we are when sadness has made its home in our mind – absorbed, engulfed by personal sorrows which we feel are those of the whole world.

'MELANCHOLY IS THE HAPPINESS OF BEING SAD.'

VICTOR HUGO

Gauguin's Lesson:
RESIST THE CALL OF SORROW

Our hearts are sometimes inclined to sadness. For some people sorrow is not so much a temptation as a vocation, a calling. Life can be so hard, how can we fail to be sad when we look at it without deliberately striving to be optimistic? Many believe – and some proclaim – that happiness is an illusion, the truth of human life is to be sad and worry is a sign of lucid realism. It's true that happiness isn't 'natural', or at any rate ceases to be so once we've left childhood behind. To some extent it then becomes an everyday struggle, or rather – let's not be overdramatic – everyday work. But does the fact that something isn't natural or easy mean we should simply give up on it, or regard it as a lie or an illusion?

As a living species, evolution has prepared us for survival by making us capable of feeling and quick to feel anger, fear and pain. But it hasn't paid too much attention to our quality of life, hence the psychic obstacles that hold us back from happiness. But this doesn't mean we should abandon the idea of living. For the temptation to be sad is itself underpinned by three major illusions.

The first is the illusion of identity, which gives us a deceptive feeling of finding or discovering ourselves through spiritual pain. Hence the immoderate attraction some teenagers feel to all that is sad or dark – we have to construct ourselves and try out all possible worlds. But once our adolescence is past, the quest for sadness merely reflects a gloomy, narcissistic little self, for in sadness we meet and rediscover nothing but ourselves. The illusion of singularity – the desire to 'feel like ourselves' – distances us from life. Where once happiness opened up the world for us, sadness separates us from it. Why do we find this preferable?

Then there is the illusion of autonomy. When sadness continues, when it ceases to be a response to external events and has its source inside us, it makes us believe we are in full control of our lives. Paradoxically, we find it reassuring to manufacture our own sadness. Whereas happiness makes us more dependent on other things in life, and we find it scary for precisely that reason.

Sadness reveals only how hard it is to live through certain times in our lives. We must listen to it without submitting to it. We are not more ourselves when we are sad and no closer to any kind of truth.

'SADNESS IS ONLY A SICKNESS
AND MUST BE BORNE LIKE A SICKNESS
WITHOUT SO MANY EXPLANATIONS
AND ARGUMENTS.'

ALAIN

The last illusion that underpins our allegiance to sadness is that of realism. This may well be the most toxic of all, though it's not entirely false. We know that people who are depressed sometimes see things more clearly than those who are not. Their gloomy eye misses none of the weaknesses and details that happier eyes skim over. But theirs is also a truncated vision. 'For in much wisdom is much grief,' says Ecclesiastes. Pessimists may be more lucid, as many scientific studies have shown, but the same studies remind us that this does not make them any better adapted to life. Absorbed in the gloomy contemplation of a world without hope or meaning, they give up the struggles of life. It can be useful to others if you talk about your pain, but that's doesn't mean you should teach them that it's a great thing or promote it as a universal truth. Great teachers of despair are legion in contemporary literature: Beckett, Cioran, Joyce, Houellebecq, Kundera or Kertész – why is our well-nourished period so keen to seize on their generalisations about the emptiness of life and happiness? Is this a legacy of Romanticism with its exaggerated penchant for promoting misery and its scorn for happiness?

Accounts of personal pain are not the problem so much as the promotion of nihilism and misanthropy. The peddlers of despair might do well to heed the words of Benjamin Constant: 'To understand human beings, it is not enough to despise them.' Such attitudes risk slowly imprisoning us inside ourselves and, ultimately, completely drying up our soul. This process is related by Romain Gary, who was no stranger to despair, but had understood that it was simply a personal, catastrophic collapse rather than a truth to be proclaimed: 'The heart of human beings fills with emptiness only when the heart itself is absent.'

Sadness, which claims to reveal the world to us, opens only one of our eyes while closing the other. Sadness is not wisdom.

Is real sadness better than fake happiness? Of course. Despite everything we've just said, sadness also contains an element of truth. The real danger lies in the unthinking adoption of a sorrowful attitude in the face of life's difficulties, its pain, trials and adversity. Crucially, it's dangerous to make sadness permanent, giving ourselves up to the slow poison of gloom. But our dark moments also have real importance.

People working on the theory of emotions note that each starts by playing a valuable role for both individuals and the species as a whole. In the animal world, of which we humans are part, sadness is a way of economising effort and so recovering from adversity. When it's temporary, turning inwards enables us to think about the causes of the sadness we feel, like an alarm alerting us to a source of pain or a lack in our lives. If this signal and the thinking it imposes on us lead us to do something about whatever it is that isn't going well and is making us suffer, then sadness has done its job to the full and we have intelligently played our part by listening to our instincts. But listening to them doesn't necessarily mean we have to obey them. Sadness is a good servant but a bad master. For while thinking about adversity is useful, ruminating on the world's badness is not. Sadness should be a transition. It can make us think, but when we adopt it as our single, chronic way of looking at things, it prevents us from seeing the beauty of life.

Sadness is simply a tool for questioning the world. We should listen to it, and then bid it goodbye. It's not something to be admired or idolised. That will just make it return all the quicker.

ENTERING THE
WINTER OF HAPPINESS

D ark days are coming. The men are bringing the cattle in for winter. They've come down from the alpine pastures and have just a few metres left to go – we can glimpse the houses on the edge of the village, just behind trees already stripped bare by the wind. The autumnal colours of the countryside still have warmth, but the wind is cold, nature is hostile and the light is fading. Down in the valley below we can see gallows on a hill overlooking the river. Country life was hard in Bruegel's day …

The painting describes both this harshness and the strength of the ordinary human beings clinging on to their lives. The returning cowherds are stocky. The man on the horse, who may be the herd's owner, is dressed in a thick coat and hat and bows his head against the biting wind. In the valley, autumn is not yet past, nor on the high ground from where we view the scene. Look carefully and you will see that some of the trees still have leaves. But it's only a matter of time. The cold will soon descend on this hamlet on the edge of winter, just as happiness will soon take its leave of us. And we will still have to keep on living.

The Return of the Herd
Pieter Bruegel the Elder (c. 1525–1569)
1565, oil on wood panel, 117 x 159 cm,
Kunsthistorisches Museum, Vienna.

This painting is one of a series of six (of which only five have survived) portraying the months of the year, following a widespread tradition derived from the mediaeval books of hours. Here Bruegel has painted the period of the first cold spells in October and November. In his day the Netherlands was subject to great tensions. Some were political – the war of liberation from Spanish domination was about to begin – others religious – Protestantism was becoming established despite the efforts of the Catholic authorities. Bruegel was politically active, a member of a Protestant group and therefore opposed to the regime of Philip II of Spain. He had fully understood that his period was entering a world of torment and confusion, a winter of the mind in which the passions and violence of the Wars of Religion were about to reign supreme.

'HAPPINESS IS THE GREATEST OF VICTORIES,
THE ONE WE WIN AGAINST THE FATE
IMPOSED UPON US.'

ALBERT CAMUS

BRUEGEL'S LESSON:
PREPARE FOR THE DEPARTURE OF HAPPINESS

The winter of happiness is coming. We have not – yet – entered misfortune, suffering and distress, but we feel an icy breath of wind that foreshadows the bitter cold to come.

Winter is not hell, but it is winter. It's cold and the days are short. Life becomes harder, the days more gloomy. We have winters of the soul in our lives too, when happiness is harder to find. At these times the happiness of plenitude is as distant as summer and we must settle for little moments of joy, snatched from the cold all around. We often experience these moments in our lives when happiness is in decline due to departure, separation, exile and endings of all kinds. Sometimes too they arrive for no apparent reason. We're still walking through the same world, but it has lost its magic. Bruegel's painting speaks to us – without over-dramatising – of all these moments when we have to survive and valiantly wait for time to pass. Here we come closer to our animal condition, when we must labour for our own survival, that of the people we care about and our society. Since the dawn of time, people have understood that the path of happiness had to pass through such winters. Where happiness is concerned some periods were ice ages, far more often governed by misery. This was true of Bruegel's time, in which the lives of the men and women he shows us were

infinitely harsh. People never – or very rarely – choose to live like that.

But we can live without happiness, although it isn't easy and we may not know how.

Should we complain? The figures in Bruegel's painting seem to accept the intermittent nature of their happiness with stoicism. They don't get upset. There's no point opening up another battlefront within and afflicting ourselves with twice the suffering by contemplating our own misfortune. Yet it's so tempting to turn difficulties into misery. Where do we draw the line between adversity, which is logical, normal and transitory, and disaster, which is repellent, abnormal and everlasting? Our reflexes often drive us to confuse the two, perhaps through the persistence of some obscure survival instinct that makes us see the danger as greater than it is so that we will deal with it more effectively.

At these times, we need the lucidity and humility to recognise that it is fear that has spoken within us, rather than intelligence.

On the subject of our human worries Cioran cruelly remarked: 'We are all jokers – we survive our problems.' Cultivating such realism in the face of adversity requires an immense amount of work. Denial ('it's not a problem') doesn't work, or not well. Lucidity ('it's only a problem'), on the other hand, is a first step towards accepting what is, without being overdramatic. We must recognise that winter has come and that for a while happiness will be difficult or impossible. We must remember that the absence of happiness is not misery and accept that unhappiness is possible, that it is foreseeable, and maybe even probable during this winter. But we must continue to live and to wait, if not to hope. We must get beyond our state of worry at the advance of winter and escape from our sadness at the death of summer.

Even if the absence of happiness makes us more fragile and worried, let's not turn our problems into misery.

How can we withstand the adversity that life hands down to us? How, despite everything, can we construct many happy moments of respite in these periods between happiness past and happiness yet to come?

The answer is by dealing with the here and now, through action and a sense of belonging, like the figures in the painting. 'Action is a series of desperate deeds that allow us to have hope,' wrote the painter Georges Braque. Not only does action change the world, it changes us too. Just as exercise warms us up in the cold, so action makes us feel the life within us.

The only hope worth having is hope that keeps us active and clear-sighted, rather than just keeping us waiting. This is hope based on the belief that happiness still exists somewhere, and that it will come back to us. It has just gone to the other side, and we have what it takes to hold out. Look at the two figures whose faces we can see, the horseman and the man with the strange bell-shaped hat. Both of them seem to be smiling. Perhaps they're already thinking of the warm fire crackling in the hearth this evening, the bowl of soup and all the talk they'll have after.

They do what they have to do in the face of adversity – act, stick together and savour any sparse remnants of happiness that come their way.

'MY ETERNAL AUTUMN, OH SEASON OF MY MIND
YOUR GROUND IS LITTERED WITH THE HANDS OF LOVERS PAST
A WIFE FOLLOWS ME, MY FATAL SHADOW
THIS EVENING THE DOVES TAKE FLIGHT FOR THE LAST TIME.'

GUILLAUME APOLLINAIRE

NIGHT
VANISHED
HAPPINESS

THE DARK NIGHT OF THE SOUL
Munch, New Snow in the Avenue

THE INCANDESCENT SOLITUDE OF PAIN
Malevich, Red Figure

STARS IN THE NIGHT
Van Gogh, Starry Night

REASONS TO FIGHT ON
Delacroix, Jacob Wrestling with the Angel

THE DARK NIGHT
OF THE SOUL

Two faceless women are walking towards us. Around them nature is icy and disturbing, the trees just dark shapes, with a scattering of snowflakes and a dull winter light over both sky and ground. And then there is the unreal whiteness of the snow-covered path, gleaming through the grey. The two women are anonymous ghosts walking out of the picture.

Where does this livid path lead? It draws our eye into the distance between the rows of black trees. What lies at the end of it? Where are these women going, towards what? Like most of Munch's paintings from this period in his life, this poses many questions, with a violence reflected in the discomfort emanating from the image. Before our eyes we see the disturbing vision of a *living* unhappiness – the trees are twisted by the wind's assault, the sparse

New Snow in the Avenue
Edvard Munch (1863–1944)
*1906, oil on canvas, 80 x 100 cm,
Munch Museum, Oslo.*

'Sickness and madness were the dark
angels watching over my cradle,' said
Munch. Deeply marked by his mother's
death from tuberculosis when he was
just five years old, he also lost a sister

to the same disease. Perhaps they have
returned here in the shape of these
two women walking into the void.
From the outset Munch's life and work
were subject to suffering, death and
desolation. He himself suffered from
anxiety, depression and alcoholism.
Misery indeed.

snowflakes spin in the icy sky. Everything is convulsed by suffering and all its uncertainties in the face of advancing misery.

This silent scene shows us every aspect of these gloomy moments in our lives, when we don't know what to do and every possible way forward seems blocked. This is precisely the dark night of the soul that Scott Fitzgerald describes in his autobiographical short story 'The Crack-Up', written four years before his death, in which he describes the depression that hit him towards the end of his life. In this winter of the heart, happiness is unthinkable. Night is falling, the two women are disappearing. Soon we will be all alone on the path.

'DO YOU UNDERSTAND?
LIFE IS PURE DESPAIR,
VERY CLEAR, DARK AND CRYSTALLINE ...
THERE IS ONLY ONE PATH THAT LEADS
THROUGH THE SNOW AND ICE OF DESPAIR.
WE MUST TAKE IT ABOVE AND BEYOND
THE ADULTERY OF REASON.'

THOMAS BERNHARD

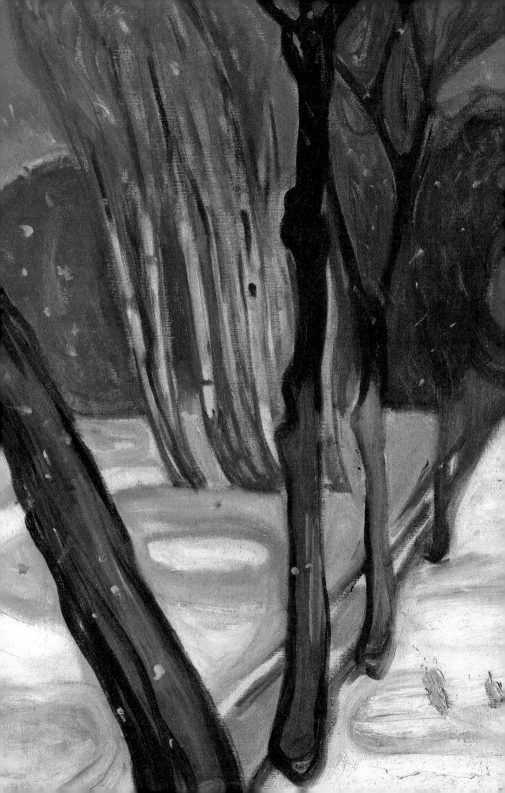

MUNCH'S LESSON:
WALK ON THROUGH THE COLD

When light has gone out of our lives and we are no longer dealing with adversity, but misery, what can we do to keep it at bay? How can we stave off despondency and keep moving? How do we fight the temptation to give up?

There are two kinds of suffering, two kinds of pain. Some, we know, will come to an end. This is the kind for which we sense there is some remedy, some solution that we can await and hope for, no matter how far off it seems. Then there's the suffering that makes us doubt, the kind that's so intense it seems to be infinite and we fear it may last for ever.

Adversity implies a way out, which we can hope for. Misery is different. It's a feeling of distress that wells up when happiness no longer seems possible or even thinkable. This does not feel like a passing, transitional state, however bad, but a permanent condition with no end in sight.

When we sense that misery has set in we fear it will last for ever. We feel lost. Wherever we look there is only darkness, emptiness and fear. How can we struggle against this?

'BENEATH MY ROBE OF VILE PURPLE, MY GOLDEN VEIL TERRIBLE TO SEE, I AM THE QUEEN OF THIS WORLD. I AM PAIN WITHOUT HOPE.'

JACQUES AUDIBERTI

We feel we are at the gates of Hell. Earthly happiness gave human beings a belief in the existence of Paradise. But misery can also convince us of the existence of Hell. This happens when we feel powerless to ward off suffering that comes at us like an advancing force, inevitably extending its grasp.

Like a vampire feeding on our fears, misery is fuelled by despair. We can't stop it oppressing us, but we can try to survive it.

What can we do? What can we hold on to in order to stop our spirit being contaminated by cold despair, which destroys us by shattering our desire to go on living? We must follow the example of the women in Munch's painting, who keep on walking through the pale light. No one knows where they're going, or even if they are walking in circles, but that doesn't matter. Walking on is all that can protect them against the sinister, death-dealing cold around them. When unhappiness advances, it's surely wiser to keep moving than to stand still.

Like a traveller lost in lands of deep cold, the main thing is to keep moving. We must keep on walking through the dark night of the soul.

'WE LONG FOR TRUTH AND FIND NOTHING IN OURSELVES BUT UNCERTAINTY. WE LOOK FOR HAPPINESS AND FIND ONLY MISERY AND DEATH.'

BLAISE PASCAL

THE INCANDESCENT
SOLITUDE OF PAIN

The silhouette of a woman, fiercely red, floats in an altered landscape. She draws our full attention, in the manner of intense suffering that admits no escape. In the background what could have been a pleasant landscape – a grassy field, a river, hills and a blue sky with clouds – is totally distorted. The sky is striped with white, the grass in the field is surrounded and stifled by thick black lines, which continue as stripes on the hills above the river. Our suffering is so great that the world around us seems transformed. It's

Red Figure
Kazimir Malevich (1878–1935)
1928-1932, oil on canvas, 30 x 25 cm,
Russian Museum, St Petersburg.

Malevich painted this picture towards the end of his life, when he was starting to suffer humiliation and persecution from Stalin's regime. He was gradually stripped of his teaching posts and all forms of official support, before being arrested in 1930 and spending a few weeks in prison. Does this painting reflect these years of unhappiness? With their apocalyptic atmosphere and depictions of humanity threatened by devastation and condemned to nihilism, Malevich's late works speak of pain and despair, but also of a will to withstand the oppressive and predatory culture that threatened the world of the peasants.

'MIDNIGHT PRECISELY.
I FEEL ALONE IN THE PRESENCE OF A DESPAIR
THAT IS STRONGER THAN ME.'

ÉMILE CIORAN

no longer the world we lived in before, the world as it's seen by the others – the people who aren't suffering.

Malevich paints a cold and terrifying world dominated by pain. The red silhouette embodies the reality of suffering. The figure is alone, as we all are in the face of misery. Always. Or is it that pain makes us believe we are alone – for who else could suffer in our place?

'THERE IS NO SUN WITHOUT SHADOW
AND WE MUST GO THROUGH THE NIGHT.'

ALBERT CAMUS

MALEVITCH'S LESSON:
REMAIN STANDING IN THE FACE OF MISERY

Misery can burn, suffocate and cut us off from life. It can kill all hope, belief, certainty and faith. It's about so much more than the pain of the present. Sadly, I have often come across it in my work as a psychotherapist. The experience of misery can be like a cancer – not satisfied with taking us over completely, distorting our vision of the world and our ability to reason, it also eats away at our memories and hopes. It makes our whole life sick.

The present is stifled by pain and gradually stripped of its content, leaving no room for anything but suffering. Unlike the time of happiness, the time of misery doesn't pass so much as drag. It seems interminable, even eternal. The future becomes hard to see and loses all meaning, weighed down with threats

'SAVE ME, O GOD;
FOR THE WATERS ARE COME IN UNTO MY SOUL.
I SINK IN DEEP MIRE, WHERE THERE IS NO STANDING:
I AM COME INTO DEEP WATERS,
WHERE THE FLOODS OVERFLOW ME.'

PSALM 69, OLD TESTAMENT

and sufferings yet to come. Psychiatrists know that, for sufferers of depression, loss of hope is an indicator of the risk of suicide.

But worst of all, perhaps, is that misery contaminates the past, making memories of happiness and moments of joy seem illusory or deceptive. Did these things even exist outside my naïve imagination? And these thoughts inject a further dose of sadness or bitterness.

All this misery advances like a slow and inevitable suffocation. It's like those dreams where we find ourselves paralysed and can't move when danger threatens. Yet we must escape this torpor and fight.

Fighting against misery means fighting the temptation to deny past happiness, and against the proud certainty of despair, which asserts that happiness will never again be possible. None of this is true. The pain of the present moment alone is real.

When it comes to facing the ordeal, the second defeat that threatens us is that of feeling lost on the inside. 'There is another sort of blow that comes from within,' wrote Scott Fitzgerald, describing his own depression. How can we preserve the possibility, deep within us, that happiness will return? How can we keep the way open for 'this passion for life that grows in great misery'? The answer is by clinging unquestioningly to life. The accounts of those who lived through the concentration camps, those most terrible places of misery, provide ultimate proof of

the intelligence of life within human beings. Here are the words of Primo Levi, who lived through hell and survived: 'I would not be able to give a full, explicit justification for this faith of mine in the future of mankind [...] It may well not be rational, but then neither is despair. It solves no problem, in fact it makes some new ones and by its very nature causes suffering.' And here are the words of Etty Hillesum, who did not survive, but whose last days were filled with an astounding hope and joy: 'My God, these times are too harsh for fragile creatures like me. After them, I know, other, more humane times will come. I should so much like to survive so I could pass on to these new times all the humanity I have preserved within me, despite the events I witness every day. This is also the only way we can prepare for the new times – by first preparing for them within ourselves.'

How can we be so proud we do not listen to the messages of our exceptional brothers and sisters in humanity? And what better reasons could there be for continuing to live, despite everything?

'WHY DO YOU CEASELESSLY MOAN,
OH MY SOUL? ANSWER ME.
WHENCE COMES THIS BURDEN OF SADNESS
NOW WEIGHING YOU DOWN?'

ALPHONSE DE LAMARTINE

STARS
IN THE NIGHT

The stars split the night with their vibrant light, sending golden tongues across the dark sky, like volcanoes rising from the depths. Below them lies a quiet village with lighted windows and all around the black shapes of the countryside and surrounding hills.

On this night of 1889, when he was working on his painting, Van Gogh may have attached candles to his hat, as he sometimes did when the darkness was too deep. The year before, he had sought to paint the night in Arles. This time he worked to capture the meeting of darkness and light in the grounds of the asylum in Saint-Rémy-de-Provence, which he had entered as a patient. When simple, everyday pleasures seem inaccessible to us, starlight is all we have left.

Sometimes we feel happiness is so far away that it no longer exists. It has been so long since we last heard its distant murmur. Should we abandon all idea of it? No. For this distant murmur, however far off it may be, is proof that happiness still exists somewhere. So we have to struggle – and not just against the external world, but against ourselves and the darkness of the soul that is rising within us. And, crucially, we must struggle not just *against*, but also *for* the light we must never forget.

Starry Night
Vincent Van Gogh (1853–1890)
1889, oil on canvas, 74 x 92 cm,
Museum of Modern Art, New York.

One night in December 1888, following
a violent row, Van Gogh threatened
his friend Gauguin – with a knife,
according to Gauguin. Theo Van Gogh,
the painter's brother, talked of the
'excessive electricity' present in the
relationship between the two artists. On
the same night, Van Gogh cut off part
of his ear and gave it to a prostitute.
Shortly afterwards he asked to be
admitted to the asylum housed in a
former Augustinian priory in Saint-

Rémy-de-Provence. In his room there,
and also in the grounds and surrounding
countryside, he worked furiously,
producing nearly 150 paintings. In the
depths of his mental night, he saw only
the brilliant light of Provence, the sun
pouring down and the magical stars.
To his brother Theo he wrote: 'And
in a painting I'd like to say something
consoling, like a piece of music. I'd like
to paint men or women with that
je ne sais quoi of the eternal, of which
the halo used to be the symbol, and
which we try to achieve through the
radiance itself, through the vibrancy
of our colorations.'

Van Gogh's Lesson:
BURSTS OF HAPPINESS
TO ESCAPE THE SHADOWS

There are strange moments when, even though we are sunk in misery, happiness bursts through and briefly takes over. Only those who have known absolute misery can describe this strange phenomenon. Imre Kertész, who escaped the concentration camps and later won the Nobel Prize for literature, told such a story in an interview: 'But yes, there was a kind of happiness in the camps, when we felt the warmth of a ray of sunlight, or a magnificent dawn rose above the camp …' Or Shukhov, hero of Alexander Solzhenitsyn's novel *One Day in the Life of Ivan Denisovich*: '[He] went to sleep fully content. He'd had many strokes of luck that day: they hadn't put him in solitary, they hadn't sent his squad to the settlement; he'd swiped a bowl of kasha at dinner; […] and he hadn't fallen ill, he'd got over it. A day without a dark cloud. Almost a happy day.'

'THE PRAYER OF A SAD MAN
DOES NOT HAVE THE STRENGTH
TO RISE UP TO GOD.'

ÉMILE CIORAN

While the strange eruption of happiness in misery may be a universal phenomenon, the lessons gleaned by those who have experienced it vary considerably. Kertész is a sombre man and a great pessimist. A little later in the interview we mentioned, he corrects the impression he gave before: 'But this happiness is worse than any misfortune ...' – although we don't have to believe him. Of course it is a poor form of happiness, but it's happiness all the same. It has the strength of living things over things that are not alive – the strength of a grass stem growing through concrete. The living will always win – grass will still be growing when there are no humans left to manufacture concrete and build motorways.

When, in the night of his misery, Van Gogh looked at the sky, he saw reasons for joy and happiness and reasons to hope and to live. Without these snatches of happiness, would he have painted so furiously?

When we are suffering, these sudden bursts of joy are like an echo of happiness, a reminder that it exists, and a reason to go on living for those enduring misery and pain.

We have adopted the lazy habit of linking suffering to creativity: artists and happiness can't go hand in hand. One of those who – involuntarily – did most to feed this myth was Vincent Van Gogh. His brother Theo wrote: 'Poor fighter and poor, poor sufferer. Nothing can be done to relieve his anguish now, but it is deep and hard for him to bear.'

Without this anguish, would Van Gogh have painted his masterpieces? We can never know. As a doctor treating mental suffering, my belief is that he would have painted differently, but still with genius. Why should we believe that his genius was fuelled only by his misery? Why, conversely, should we not think that he was inspired by his dreams of happiness, whether it was attained or not? Why is it so hard for us to see that the elements of light are much more intense and more numerous in his work than those of shadow? It was his passionate love of life and happiness that drove Van Gogh to paint, not his misery. He spent his life repeating that his suffering was a hindrance. Even on his deathbed when, in response to encouragement from his brother Theo and Dr Gachet, he replied, semi-conscious, 'It's no good, I will be sad my whole life', he did not see any value in his pain, only that it was impossible for him to keep fighting.

We are more than our suffering. We should not look to it for truth or lessons. Let's look to our light rather than our darkness.

'BY REASON OF THE VOICE OF MY GROANING
MY BONES CLEAVE TO MY SKIN.
I AM LIKE A PELICAN OF THE WILDERNESS:
I AM LIKE AN OWL OF THE DESERT.'

PSALM 102, OLD TESTAMENT

Gradually, misery kills our belief that connection can heal and save us. Suffering leads to isolation, and the natural, perverse effect of painful emotions is to distance us from others. In its least serious form it leads to the navel-gazing of ruminations on our sadness; at its more serious, it is the trauma of those who have survived disasters or extreme pain and now feel forever different from other people. But here again, just because this aspect of suffering is universal, it doesn't mean we have to accept it. Besides, its consequences are not always the same. Some people abandon themselves to the gloomy joys of their painful loneliness and indulge in the puerile pleasure of feeling alone and misunderstood. But others realise that such renunciation only increases the power of an alienating and unwanted misery.

Van Gogh wanted connection just as he wanted happiness. But both these things were always hard for him, other than through his art. There are many details of his life that reflect his aspiration to be sociable. While he was living in Arles he went to great lengths to get himself adopted by the inhabitants and he bought twelve chairs for his house, hoping to gather a community of painters who would be united like the twelve apostles.

'IT DOESN'T TAKE EVERYTHING TO MAKE A WORLD
IT TAKES HAPPINESS, AND THAT'S ALL.'

PAUL ÉLUARD

Where did he get this vocation from? Vincent's father was a pastor and in his youth the painter studied theology and tried unsuccessfully to be a preacher. Vincent's letters show that he was a profoundly good man, sincerely concerned to share happiness: 'We must paint nature's rich and magnificent aspects; we need good cheer and happiness, hope and love …'; 'I'd like to say something consoling, like a piece of music. […] To express hope through some star. The ardour of a living being through the rays of a setting sun.'

In extreme adversity, the worst logic and the greatest temptation is that of isolation. Of course our fight against misery must often be conducted alone, but our capacity for happiness can only survive through connection and the desire for connection.

Misery must not lead us into solitude. When we isolate ourselves we further destroy our chances of happiness and its future rebirth.

REASONS TO
FIGHT ON

Head down, Jacob hurls himself into the fight with all his might. Who is his opponent, and what is this brawl all about? He doesn't know. All he knows is that he is alone, having helped his entire clan, his family and servants to ford the River Jabbok. He is the only one left behind on the bank. Again Jacob leaps at his opponent. The angel – which the fighting man, blinkered by his down-turned eyes, can't see for what it is – reels slightly under the shock, but holds steady. Look at Jacob's muscled torso,

Jacob Wrestling with the Angel (detail)
Eugène Delacroix (1798–1863)
1855–1861, oil and wax on plaster, 750 x 485 cm, Church of Saint-Sulpice, Chapelle des Saints-Anges, Paris.

This vast fresco is Delacroix's spiritual testament. It can be admired in the half-light of the Church of Saint-Sulpice in Paris. In the last years of his life, Delacroix withdrew from the high-society life in which he had been a prominent figure and, despite his age and ill-health, devoted himself entirely to this last commission. The writer Maurice Barrès noted that the painting was 'a supreme, autobiographical work, summing up the experience of a great life, a final testament written by the old artist on the wall of the Angels.' At the bottom right of the painting Delacroix has composed a true still life, harmoniously arranging all the equipment Jacob has left on the ground in order to fight for his life more freely. Shortly after he had painted it, the artist too put down his brushes. It was perhaps his final epitaph.

his stubborn forehead lowered like a bull's. Look at the straight severe face of the angel, its feet firmly grounded, shaken but still solidly withstanding the man's violent assault. In the morning the angel realises that Jacob won't let himself be beaten and strikes him on the hip. The violent blow dislocates Jacob's femur and at last opens his eyes. He understands what is happening and asks his divine adversary to bless him. The angel asks his name, then tells him, 'Thy name shall be called no more Jacob, but Israel: for as a prince hast thou power with God and with men, and hast prevailed.' (According to the exegetes, Israel means 'May God prove strong' or 'He who fights with God'.) Jacob limps from the fight, injured but blessed. Transfigured.

When everything around us has given way, the last battle takes place within us. We must confront doubt, nihilism, resignation and the temptation to give in. But when it comes to it, why should we fight? Why not just go under? Of course, we have a vague sense that giving up the fight means giving up life. But it's so hard to battle on, without hope.

'THE QUEST FOR HAPPINESS IN THIS LIFE
IS WHERE THE REAL SPIRIT OF REBELLION LIES.'
HENRIK IBSEN

DELACROIX'S LESSON:
FIGHT TO ENABLE HAPPINESS TO BE REBORN

Cunning, sly and powerful, Jacob was an exceptional 'living machine', to borrow Paul Valéry's term. But where can we common mortals find the strength to fight on alone through the night, not knowing the meaning of the struggle or what its outcome will be? We often see this kind of thing in psychiatry, when we're treating people for depression. They've been deserted by what we call the 'vital impulse' and just keep on saying, 'I can't go on.' It's not a wish to die that draws them towards non-existence, so much as a weariness with life and its constant efforts. Like a shipwrecked sailor who stops swimming, or a dying person who gives up the struggle, they are exhausted. Of course action without hope can sometimes seem absurd in material terms – it won't necessarily change anything.

But action is always life-saving at a psychological level. It gives meaning to the present and a foothold to our survival. It channels our energies and draws a line around our temptation to despair.

The temptation to see meaning in adversity is always there. In another passage from the Bible, the righteous Job is subjected to the worst misfortunes. The three friends who visit him are sure that he must have done something wrong to deserve such punishment and try to persuade him this is true. But Job gets angry with them – he knows he has done nothing wrong. This obsession with finding a hidden meaning to the misfortunes that befall us is a slippery slope that has led many astray in the field of psychology. Fritz Zorn, in his autobiography *Mars*, describes how, in his view, his stifling education was the source of his cancer. He then began to see his illness as a liberation, as though it could enable him to escape his gloomy existence. Today such theories and beliefs about the psycho-somatic transformation of misfortune and misery are disputed. Not that it never happens, but often it is no more than one mechanism among many and very seldom the only one.

There may be no discernible meaning to suffering. At best it may prove to have been useful with hindsight, and then only if we use it to draw lessons for the future, in order to improve our lives, or those of others.

Jacob was profoundly changed by his night of combat. Are we really changed by misfortune? Undoubtedly so, and in two ways: it makes us different from what we were before, and from what others still are, if they have not experienced what we have gone through.

'AFFLICTION IS A MULE:
IT IS STUBBORN AND STERILE.'
VICTOR HUGO

But the real question we need to ask is whether misery is better at changing human beings than happiness. Often it marks us more deeply, not because it is misery, but because it seems less acceptable to us. This idea was expressed by the poet Raymond Radiguet, author of *Devil in the Flesh*: 'Misery is inadmissible. Happiness alone seems rightful.' But this is to look at the transfiguring power of adversity from the wrong angle. Perhaps it is not misfortune that transforms us, so much as our fight against it. Perhaps we are enriched by the experience and memory of the fight, rather than of our suffering. This was the view expressed by the radiant Etty Hillesum in her journal: 'We must be tougher, not harder.'

It's the struggle against misfortune, and only this, that can teach us and make us grow. Not misfortune itself, which only makes us hard.

One of misfortune's countless dangers is of course the annihilation of our being, be it physical, through illness or suicide, or mental, through depression. But they also include bitterness, cynicism and constant negativity in our view of life, both our own and that of others. The experience of misery can drive us to find everything ridiculous and pointless, even happiness and the quest for it.

So we absolutely have to fight, both on the outside and on the inside of ourselves, in order to preserve the return of happiness, to make it possible for us to be happy again and make others happy, one day, in the future. This is no small task. When we are sunk deep in misery, we have to make a huge effort to accept that happiness still exists, absolutely and in the lives of others all around us.

For the greatest victory of misfortune would be to make us abandon the idea of happiness and contaminate our soul with bitterness and cynicism, which are the only things that can prevent the return and rebirth of happiness over the long term.

DAWN
THE RETURN
OF HAPPINESS

HAPPINESS GROWS STRONGER
Bonnard, The Almond Tree in Blossom

HAPPINESS REGAINED
Courbet, The Beach at Palavas

HAPPINESS IS A LONG STORY
Rembrandt, The Return of the Prodigal Son

THE WISDOM OF HAPPINESS
Chardin, The Silver Goblet

ETERNAL HAPPINESS?
Spilliaert, October Evening

HAPPINESS
GROWS STRONGER

A n almond tree blossoms in an explosion of whiteness, every spring the same, jostling the sky and pushing it back to the edges of the canvas. This unfinished painting is Bonnard's last work. It was on his easel when he died. His family described how he was working on it right up to the last moment, and particularly the ground under the olive tree: 'This green, on this bit of ground bottom left, it's no good. It needs yellow …'

The Almond Tree in Blossom
Pierre Bonnard (1867–1947)
1947, oil on canvas, 55 x 37 cm,
Musée national d'art moderne, Paris.

Unlike Van Gogh, Bonnard was an artist recognised in his lifetime and happy in his period. He went on painting with pleasure until his last days, despite his advanced age. Every year he was always moved by spring, and his final spring was exceptional. The almond tree stood outside his bedroom window at his house in Le Cannet and 'perhaps never before had the tree put on such a magnificent gown as it did that spring, as though it wanted to promise him fine days to come', as one of his biographers put it. This painting, as simple and luminous as the almond tree itself, reminds us of the fundamental lesson of happiness: it isn't located in the future, or in the past, but in the present of life.

The almond tree is the first to flower at the end of winter. Its blossom bursts forth impatiently, heralding the return of spring. So here it is, the spring that astonishes us every time. And what astonishes us even more is that it comes back – we always feel an animal wonder at its return and presence, as though each spring is always better than the last, as though this eternal starting-over has a cumulative effect on our happiness. We feel as though all these cycles and eclipses exist solely to enhance our inner instinct for happiness, and our belief in its necessity. If we are more and more amazed by spring every year, this is surely because our understanding of happiness has grown, and because we see things with greater acuity. We are more able to go straight to what matters most – to the simple happiness of being alive.

'PARADISE IS NOT ON EARTH,
BUT THERE ARE PIECES OF IT.'
JULES RENARD

BONNARD'S LESSON:
INCREASE THE INTELLIGENCE OF OUR HAPPINESS

We are once more feeling happy, after having not been happy at all. After a journey through pain, suffering, problems, sorrow and greyness, we stop, breathe and smile. We fill up our senses with sounds, smells, light and colour. We feel life inside us and around us, just like before.

We start to hope again, and to believe that this happiness of today will still be here tomorrow. We rediscover our infinite potential for happiness.

Life can be difficult, the world can be hard and brutal. This is why happiness has to avoid the two pitfalls of naïvety ('I'll be happy if I do what is right')

and blindness ('everything is for the best in the best of all possible worlds'). This is also why lasting happiness – which is not permanent, but a regular repetition of occurrences – is a form of wisdom, the 'maximum happiness with the maximum of lucidity' that André Comte-Sponville talked about. This wisdom without illusions involves, among other things, understanding that happiness is not just important, but it is vital.

We must put our heart and intelligence into the pursuit of happiness, using each of its eclipses to think about its nature and why it returns so regularly. We must enable our instinct for happiness to grow throughout our lives.

Grow older and be happy? That's not so easy. Age can also bring bitterness. It's only too easy to see how bitterness, regret and cynicism may tempt us as our bodies and hearts become worn. It might seem that happiness depends on the freshness of youth. But fortunately for the older among us and unfortunately for the younger, things are a bit more complicated. The sap of the tree of happiness consists not of youth, but of life itself.

The intelligence of life belongs to those who accept the passing of time and who continue to enjoy the time that's here now. And this is also the intelligence of happiness.

HAPPINESS
REGAINED

The traveller has returned to look at the sea. He has walked quite a distance, not in an aimless way, but knowing exactly what he is looking for. He isn't surprised by what he sees, which clearly makes it even more powerful. We are witnessing the sober, contained happiness of a reunion. His most elegant gesture of greeting expresses complicity ('Here we are, together once more'), joy ('At last!'), humility ('I am

The Beach at Palavas
Gustave Courbet (1819–1877)
1854, oil on canvas, 39 x 46 cm,
Musée Fabre, Montpellier.

Gustave Courbet is often presented as the foremost painter of Realism, the man who turned the page on Idealism and Romanticism to paint the human comedy warts and all. He's remembered as a politically active artist supported by Proudhon, a socialist who helped to demolish the Vendôme Column commemorating Napoleon and spent four years of his life in prison. But there is another facet to his life and work. This huge, boastful man, who loved to hunt and was an early ecologist, was also a lover and painter of nature. In this picture of a beach, as in many of his works, he salutes the immensity and beauty of the planet with the same emotion and freedom he shows his social subjects. Perhaps he needed to draw strength from the contemplation of nature and a return to the simple, fundamental happiness of our animal roots.

'BEING HAPPY MEANS HAVING OVERCOME
THE ANXIETY OF HAPPINESS.'

MAURICE MAETERLINCK

tiny next to you') and also just a little bit of pride. Without this little man and his happy gesture, this painting would lose all its charm and meaning.

Why is happiness regained sometimes stronger and more intense than emerging happiness? Is it because we get used to things so quickly, because with time happiness starts to lose its savour? Is it because separations and interruptions make our happiness seem more valuable to us, opening our eyes to its real value?

To enhance our awareness of happiness, we sometimes need it to go away. It may be that its intermittence is in fact a subtle necessity.

'I WILL NOW DESCRIBE THE EXPERIENCE
OF WONDERING AT THE EXISTENCE
OF THE WORLD BY SAYING: IT IS THE EXPERIENCE
OF SEEING THE WORLD AS A MIRACLE.'

LUDWIG WITTGENSTEIN

Courbet's Lesson:
'This Moment is a Moment of Happiness'

I know this beach at Palavas, painted by Courbet. In fact, I know it very well. It was where I spent all my childhood summers. My grandfather had built a hut there and as soon as we arrived on the first day of the holidays, I would run to the dunes and climb up to look at the sea.

Much later I went back there with a friend who was very ill. We sat down on the sand to watch the waves. It was late afternoon. My mind kept returning to the painful thought of her impending death in waves of anxiety and sorrow. But the movement of the sea kept pulling me back to the present moment, in other words to her life, and this precise moment where we were together looking at the horizon.

There was nothing poetic about all this, because my friend was suffering and the illness that was eating at her body had begun to cloud her mind. So there was no poetry, just a terrifying intensity – a kind of hardness and grandeur in the human condition that was completely beyond our grasp. The sound of the waves merged into the tumult of our thoughts, caught between past and present, life and death, peace and pain. Despite the illness within her, my friend tried to take in as much as she could of this moment, which was still somehow a moment of happiness, whatever was about to happen. A few days later she was dying in the summer heat of the Languedoc. It's often said that we should remember our dead only in their moments of life and happiness.

So is this what happiness is? Being able to say to ourselves, whatever happened before, whatever will happen next, it was worth being alive just for this moment.

Courbet's greeting to the sea is such a sublime little gesture. It says: 'I know you, I love you, I honour you – and I'm so happy!'

And he was absolutely right to celebrate this moment, bringing it to life with his brushes for all to see, just as we are absolutely right to be aware of each of our moments of happiness, and to name them.

There is a magic phrase, like the ones made up by children, one single phrase we should say to ourselves each time happiness comes our way, and it's simply this: 'This moment is a moment of happiness.'

In expressing our awareness of happiness and gratitude for it, we attain a kind of eternity. This happiness will not last for ever, but it will remain forever true that we experienced this moment. Some would say, why make so much effort to be conscious of feeling happiness? Won't this spoil its essence, which is to be immaterial and intangible? Why put such subtle, volatile sensations into words, which are necessarily clumsy and deceptive? The answer is simple: because living isn't just about feeling; it's also about creating our own world. In Genesis, God names what he creates, and by naming things and creatures he gives them life. We are clearly not gods, but we are the demiurges of our own happiness. Demiurges don't create, but they do organise. As André Comte-Sponville reminds us, a demiurge is an 'artisan god, skilful rather than perfect'.

And so it is with our own lives. We don't just receive happiness, we can also make it. Sometimes it's harmonious and sometimes it's a bit wobbly. There's no point emulating the artists and trying to be innovative, unique or admirable.

Let us just be the artisans of our own happiness.

'FOR INDEED, WITH HARDSHIP
WILL BE EASE.
INDEED, WITH HARDSHIP
WILL BE EASE.'

SURA 94, THE QUR'AN

HAPPINESS
IS A
LONG STORY

ood Lord, where has he been? He looks like a galley slave or a convict with that shaved head, and look at his bare feet inside those worn-out shoes. The prodigal son has returned – the one who set off to waste his share of the inheritance 'with riotous living' 'in a far country'. Soon he will be describing how he fed the swine and was often so poor and hungry he would have eaten their food. When he came back he was afraid of being rejected, taunted

The Return of the Prodigal Son
Rembrandt Van Rijn (1606–1669)
c. 1669, oil on canvas, 262 x 206 cm,
Hermitage Museum, St Petersburg.

This work of imposing size is Rembrandt's last painting. More than just a famous episode from the Gospels, here Rembrandt conveys the deeper meaning of a human story through a gesture of love and forgiveness. The father's face, on which time has left only the trace of light, expresses serenity and an absolute gift of self. Is this attitude of total trust a symbolic representation of the painter's state of mind, having become reconciled with himself on the threshold of death? This picture was painted during the last year of his life, when his star was fading and he was living a frugal existence, focused on spirituality. His son Titus had died a few years before.

'Love truth,
but pardon error.'

Voltaire

and criticised. His brother and the other members of the household, whom we glimpse in the shadows, were ready to do just that. But his father was the first to react, and he was seized by happiness. It was he who ran up to his son, who had been afraid to approach him, and, so the Gospel tells us, 'fell on his neck, and kissed him'. This is an exceptional attitude for a Biblical father to take towards his son. It is an exceptional moment. It is also an exceptional lesson in love and intelligence. 'For this my son was dead, and is alive again; he was lost, and is found.' Their embrace is lit up in a golden light. The son's eyes are closed; he is pressed against his father like the child he once was, which he is again at this moment, suddenly realising the immense love his father has for him. All those mistakes, all that suffering, and at the end of it – because we were and still are loved – forgiveness and happiness.

Rembrandt's Lesson :
LIVE IN PEACE WITH YOURSELF AND OTHERS

The road to happiness is littered with mistakes. So much wasted time, effort, anger and despair. But there's no point looking back. This long, long path to happiness that never quite arrives gradually teaches us the most important things about ourselves and the meaning of our lives. For the story of our happiness consists of our mistakes, sufferings and wanderings. They are what give it its own particular identity, texture and character among all the individual happinesses of human beings. And they almost certainly give it its savour, if we know how to see and take in the accidents we encounter on the way with the tenderness of a father seeing and taking in the son who has returned to him.

So much happiness wasted, but we mustn't regret it. That would be doubly painful, adding present pain to that of the past. A great deal of research has been done into the psychology of regret. We know that the power of regret is always attenuated by the intensity of our experience of the present. Even if we have failed or not achieved our aims, if we have done something fully and truly we will regret it less. We also know that we will have fewer regrets about our actions than about our inaction. In the long term there are almost always fewer regrets at having acted and failed than not having tried at all. There are many reasons why, but the most important is this: action can lead to happiness, at least in the moment. Not acting brings only calm or guilt.

These are all reasons to accept our past in all its aspects. We don't have to approve of it, but we should accept it. And in doing so we should practise the art of discernment. I need to understand what elements of my own history and journey I would like to see reappear, and what I never want to see again.

To cultivate our happiness, we must direct our efforts to the present, enriching it with our past, rather than weighing down or blocking it with things that are gone. We must make peace with ourselves. This is one key to happiness.

This elderly father has understood that there was no time to waste on reproaches, remonstrations, punishments or reprisals. Misfortune and trials are enough. We can and should draw lessons from them, but also, and crucially, once our trials are over, we must rebuild a serenity of soul. Diderot said: 'The only duty

'DEPENDING ON WHAT HAS HAPPENED,
TO FORGIVE IS TO ABANDON THE IDEA
OF PUNISHING OR HATING,
AND SOMETIMES ALSO OF JUDGING.'

ANDRÉ COMTE-SPONVILLE

is to be happy.' He undoubtedly meant to remind us that, even if it isn't our only duty, it is certainly first among them. And once pain is past, the most urgent need is for soothing and happiness, before resentment and perhaps even before analysis and understanding. Often this involves forgiveness, of others and also of ourselves. For without it there will be bitterness and anger, however righteous, and it's not always worth devoting our time and energy to such things. A human life contains as many opportunities for forgiveness as for hatred, each one a crossroads between an excess of misery and the rebirth of happiness. Suffering must surely make us blind, since we get it wrong so often.

Yet the evidence is there in front of our eyes. Rembrandt's painting speaks to us of the urgent need for all possible forms of forgiveness.

Look at the infinite gentleness of this father's face, the tender, protective gesture of his hands on his son's shoulders. One repents, the other forgives. One trusts to mercy and the other gives it. In this moment, which of the two is the happier?

THE WISDOM
OF HAPPINESS

A silver goblet, three apples, a bowl containing a spoon with its back to us and two chest-nuts, all placed on a stone shelf. Together they form a simple, beautiful whole, in a muted, slightly eerie light. The objects abandoned for a moment in a dimly lit corner are shown *in majesty*, as is said of some depictions of Christ or the Virgin Mary.

The Silver Goblet
Jean Siméon Chardin (1699–1779)
1768, oil on canvas, 33 x 41 cm,
Musée du Louvre, Paris.

Chardin became a member of the French Academy at a very young age, but only in the minor category of 'skill with animals and fruit'; in other words, so-called 'genre' scenes and still lifes, at a time when large historical works were most valued. Chardin's life was like his paintings – ordinary to the point of being enigmatic. The art of this smooth man enchanted the greatest of his contemporaries. Diderot said of him: 'This is the artist who hears the harmony of colours and reflections. Oh Chardin! What you mix on your palette is not white, red or black, but the very substance of objects; you catch air and light on the end of your brush and attach them to the canvas.' Chardin has no rival in rendering the substance of everyday life in all its happy plenitude.

'ETERNAL LIFE BELONGS TO THOSE
WHO LIVE IN THE PRESENT.'

LUDWIG WITTGENSTEIN

This is not a perfect still life, such as those painted by many Dutch masters in the preceding century – works that are sufficient unto themselves, proud of their technical perfection and asking nothing of the viewer except, perhaps, to admire their technical perfection. Chardin was after something more than that kind of realism. He wanted us to open our eyes. For him imitation was a means rather than an end. This painting teaches us to see the secret, silent life of things. It encourages us to meditate. Indeed, Chardin's style has been described as a 'meditated art', and this is exactly right.

This art holds us in the present, in the poetry, force and life of the present moment – in other words, in the antechamber of our happiness.

'WE HAVE NOTHING TO FEAR FROM THE GODS.
WE HAVE NOTHING TO FEAR FROM DEATH.
WE CAN BEAR SUFFERING.
WE CAN ATTAIN HAPPINESS.'

DIOGENES

Chardin's Lesson:
TAKE STRENGTH FROM
HAPPY STILLNESS

We have been through so many adventures on our road to happiness! Now we have almost reached our destination – though of course it's only a stopover, we'll be on our way again soon. But not right now. We have changed in the course of our journey. Like characters in the Zen tales, we now know the importance of some details, the effects of anodyne gestures, the savour of tiny moments and the power of unobtrusive objects.

At last we know that happiness can spring from almost nothing at all, from things we never used to notice. Though we didn't know it then, we were blind.

Now we also understand that happiness is an ideal that we can at best try gently to approach, rather than a tyrannical, exhausting absolute that we absolutely must attain and possess right now. This is why the wisdom of happiness is above all about practice rather than knowledge, as Montaigne noted in his *Essays*: 'We can be knowledgeable with other men's knowledge but we cannot be wise with other men's wisdom.'

The practice of happiness is akin to patiently working in the garden of our soul, or like learning a musical instrument. Every day we must make a little light effort, so that every now and then we will feel the weight of moments of grace.

The more we practise these exercises, the more often everything lights up and takes flight. People have always known the 'recipes' for happiness – establish the basic material conditions, welcome little moments of happiness, gently and regularly avoid little moments of unhappiness, and hold on to life when misfortune strikes. This practice is simple, but it isn't easy. Yet gradually, as we experience the birth and rebirth of happiness, we see that it has fewer and fewer requirements, and we are more and more able to give it a place in our life and our soul.

This developing ability to feel happiness more easily is known as 'mind training'.

Knowing how to recognise and welcome happiness is an art in itself and a form of wisdom, as we have just recalled. But how can we prevent the absence of happiness causing us suffering? Meditation can help. Cautiously and patiently, science and medicine are now starting to study the use of meditation, not as a way of thinking deeply about a particular subject – which is what meditation means in the Western tradition – but as an act of presence to the world, as it is in the Eastern tradition. In psychotherapy we use this type of meditation with our patients as one form of treatment that can help them avoid sinking back into depression. These exercises involve keeping the mind in the present moment without passing any kind of judgement on what is happening around and inside us. We just accept what comes and gently return to the present moment each time our mind wanders elsewhere, into pain, regrets or criticisms. So painting is useful in meditation. Though it has less power to generate strong emotions than music or reading, it is better at arousing our subtler feelings and a serene connection to the world.

What exactly is the relationship between meditation and happiness? Both teach us to live in the present rather than in a past we may regret or long for, or a future we may fear or eagerly await. Many people never experience their happiness in the present, but only retrospectively, as Raymond Radiguet indicates: 'Happiness, I knew you only / By the sound you made as you left.' The intensity of our presence to the world

enhances our capacity for happiness. Meditation helps us be more present, but it also helps us not to pile up painful feelings at times when we are not happy, or are unhappy. We must accept both happiness and its absence. The goal of meditation is serenity rather than placidity, distance rather than detachment. Its role is not to replace action, but to precede and follow action – and for its most gifted practitioners, to accompany action. Meditation does not seek to suppress the anxiety of happiness, or even to struggle against it, but to integrate and dissolve it in happiness itself.

Meditation helps us expand our relationship with happiness, allowing it to nourish us, rather than simply seeking to enjoy it.

Let's go back to Jean Siméon Chardin, his painting and his genius, and to the paused time and light-hearted depth he invites us to experience. Let's meditate on his picture. Some days, when our lives allow it, we can feel an inner peace, like an echo of the 'peace of objects' that gently reigns in this small masterpiece. And it also echoes the much greater peace of the world around us, whether it be real, possible or just a dream. It's like an awakening of the 'oceanic feeling' that the first psychoanalysts saw as a form of regression, but which we now sense may offer a glimpse of a higher state of consciousness. Thanks to Chardin's painting, we are no longer merely looking, admiring, or even meditating. We are absorbed, without trying to understand, act or think. The boundary between us and the painting has blurred. We are in the painting. We are the painting. We have slipped quietly into contemplation. Here is André Comte-Sponville's definition of contemplation, by far the best in my view: 'Knowing what is, without trying to use, possess or judge it. The peak of spiritual life, where the self dissolves in the contemplation of its object.'

Psychologists are also very interested in researching the contemplative approach. It is the only attitude offering access to the invisible through the body. No one has ever seen love, the infinite or serenity. Observation, intuition and reflective thought enable us to assume that these things exist, but contemplation enables us to know, or at least to sense, them.

Contemplation gives us access to one of the fundamental aspects of happiness: the dissolution of the self, or rather its infinite expansion. When we are happy we become one with everything – some would say, with God.

'IN ETERNITY THERE IS INDEED SOMETHING TRUE
AND SUBLIME. BUT ALL THESE TIMES AND PLACES
AND OCCASIONS ARE NOW AND HERE.
GOD HIMSELF CULMINATES IN THE PRESENT MOMENT
AND WILL NEVER BE MORE DIVINE IN THE LAPSE
OF THE AGES.'

HENRY DAVID THOREAU

ETERNAL
HAPPINESS?

Shadow, light and mystery. All of Spilliaert's strange art is distilled into this large pastel drawing of a figure walking through an unreal or non-existent space. She is leaning forward slightly. Is she in a hurry? Where is there to hurry to? Or is she bent with weariness? Where can she have come from? The scene is filled with a dazzling, hot, yellow light, so strong that it transforms the figure into a walking shadow and so dense it looks like rain. Léon Spilliaert was a reserved, secretive man who may have drawn inspiration for this drawing from his long evening walks on the beaches of his home town of Ostend. Where others would see only a woman walking against the light, perhaps he realised that something very particular was happening just at that moment. Perhaps it was like an illumination, the dazzling light revealing a transition or a materialisation of the border between two worlds. Life and death, perhaps? Happiness also lies between two worlds – the material world that provides the conditions for its emergence and the spiritual world towards which it draws us. It is also a transition, but to what? It is an antechamber, but of what? What are we moving towards when our soul reaches for happiness? This picture gives no answers, just the dazzling light of happiness.

October Evening
Léon Spilliaert (1881–1946)
1912, pastel and coloured pencil on card,
70 x 90 cm, Spilliaert collection, Brussels.

'I have a dazzling memory of my childhood, until the day I was sent to school. After that my soul was stolen and I never got it back. This painful quest sums up the whole story of my painting.' It's easy to imagine Spilliaert strolling across the beaches of Ostend in his nostalgic search for the happiness of childhood. All of his work expresses the quiet melancholy of a solitary man who always preferred to draw in pencil, pastels and Indian ink, materials reflecting his own fundamental fragility.

'WHENEVER DEATH COMES,
IT WILL FIND ME STILL HAPPY.'
MARCUS AURELIUS

Spilliaert's Lesson :
LIVE HAPPILY TO LOSE THE FEAR OF DEATH

Happiness is a form of transcendence that often leads us to the borderline between two worlds. It suspends time and brings plenitude or the forgetting of self, an awareness of connectedness and belonging to something that is beyond us or all-encompassing. Happiness can sometimes have lightness, but it is always deep – sometimes dizzyingly so. We are aware of it in moments, and in those moments we understand that its role goes far beyond the slight increase in our comfort or sense of well-being to which its detractors seek to confine it.

Happiness is a tool for understanding the world in its most joyous and most mysterious aspects.

What's the point of living if one day you're going to die? Surely happiness is laughable when we know how every human life will end. So what's the point of it? This question has only one possible answer: happiness is the antidote to the painful, unbearable awareness of our mortality. Of all the animals, we are the only ones

'THE EARTHLY PARADISE
IS WHERE I AM.'

VOLTAIRE

to know that one day we will die. How can we bear this idea, and still keep on living? Through happiness. Happiness is the only remedy for our fear of death that remains effective over the long-term. It doesn't remove our fear by repressing it, as we sometimes do when we seek refuge in action or distraction. But it teaches us to accept it.

We must be happy, because death exists.

The lives of our ancestors were so hard that they had to invent a place where happiness might be possible, an elsewhere from which human beings had long ago been expelled, and of which they could dream. The idea of Paradise reflected the desire for a happiness that, though deferred, was perfect and eternal, granted to those whose lives were hard and uncertain. It was a fine idea, an extraordinary promise. Sometimes we still

believe in it. But today another dream has appeared alongside that of Paradise, and that is the dream of happiness. This development is no coincidence. As we have seen, happiness enables us to fill ourselves with a rush of eternity during which time stands still and we seem to be immortal. Everything that Paradise promised us tomorrow, happiness brings us today. These magical moments give us a tangible experience of what Paradise might be, if it exists, and also of what immortality might be: fearing nothing of what is to come. A moment of happiness is a breath of Paradise.

Every time we are happy, we are immortal. Paradise is here and now.

'JOY THAT IS THE SAME
AS CERTAINTY AND ENOUGH,
WITHOUT FURTHER EVIDENCE,
TO MAKE ME INDIFFERENT TO DEATH.'

MARCEL PROUST

TAKING FLIGHT IN THE GREAT WIND OF THE WORLD...

I t's probably a dream – or a memory emerging from childhood, or out of nowhere. The clouds pass, blown along by the wind. The sky is bright, the air is warm. A woman stands there with a parasol over her shoulder, looking into the distance. We can see nothing of her face. Who is she? And you, who are you exactly? Is this woman you? Your

Study of a Figure Outdoors: Woman with a Parasol Facing Left
Claude Monet (1840–1926)
1886, oil on canvas, 131 x 88 cm, Musée d'Orsay, Paris.

The Île aux Orties at the mouth of the River Epte was where Monet kept his boats, notably his studio boat. One day, as he was coming back from painting, he caught sight of Suzanne, daughter of his partner Alice, standing on the riverbank. For him it was a like a vision, the return of a forgotten memory of his dead wife Camille. Over the following days he went back to the same place with Suzanne, to capture this impression from life. He painted two pictures, one facing right and the other – seen here – facing left. Did he paint a girl of eighteen, or the memory of his wife? In 1886 Monet had been living in Giverny for three years, and he would stay there until his death. This was the period of the last exhibition by the Impressionist group. It was also one of the last times that Monet painted a human figure (already blurred here), before concentrating on variations on themes from nature. He announced this himself, saying of this painting: 'I'm working as never before, and trying new things, figures outdoors as I understand them, done like landscapes.'

mother? Your grandmother? Or are you in the clouds, flying in the wind? Perhaps you are a blade of grass. What's happening? Are you being born, or dying? What will happen now?

None of this matters. In reality, all that matters is that this moment is a moment of happiness. Just a little happiness, in the great wind of the world.

'I HAVE SET BEFORE THEE AN OPEN DOOR,
AND NO MAN CAN SHUT IT.'

THE BOOK OF REVELATION

SELECTED READING

On happiness

- André C., *Vivre heureux. Psychologie du Bonheur*, Paris, Odile Jacob, 2003.
- Cloninger, C.R., *Feeling Good. The Science of Well-Being*, Oxford, Oxford University Press, 2004.
- Comte-Sponville A. *Dictionnaire philosophique*, Paris, Presses Universitaires de France, 2001.
- Comte-Sponville A., *Le Bonheur, désespérément*, Nantes, Pleins Feux, 2000.
- Comte-Sponville A., *Traité du désespoir et de la beatitude*, Paris, Presses Universitaires de France, 1984.
- De Botton A., *The Consolations of Philosophy*, London, Penguin, 2001.
- Emmons R.A., McCullough M.E., *The Psychology of Gratitude*, Oxford, Oxford University Press, 2004.
- Epicurus, *The Art of Happiness*. Trans. John K. Strodach, London, Penguin, 2013.
- Haidt J., *The Happiness Hypothesis. Finding modern truth in ancient wisdom*, New York, Basic Books, 2006.
- Hanson R., *Hardwiring Happiness. How to reshape your brain and your life*, London, Rider Books, 2014.
- Kahneman D., Diener E., Schwartz N. (eds), *Well-Being. The foundations of hedonic psychology*, New York, Russell Sage Foundation, 1999.
- Legrenzi P., *Le Bonheur*, Brussels, De Boeck, 2001.
- Mauzi R., *L'Idée du bonheur dans la littérature et la pensée française au XVIIIe siècle*, Geneva, Slatkine Reprints, 1979.
- McMahon D.M., *Happiness. A history*, New York, Atlantic Monthly Press, 2006.
- Myers D.G., *The Pursuit of Happiness*, New York, Avon Books, 1992.
- Snyder C.R., Lopez S.J. (eds), *Handbook of Positive Psychology*. Oxford, Oxford University Press, 2002.
- Van Rillaer J., *La Gestion de soi*, Brussels, Mardaga, 1992.

On painting and the works discussed

- Adhémar H., *Catalogue de l'exposition* Hommage à Claude Monet, Paris, Éditions de la RMN, 1980.
- Battisti E., *Giotto*, Geneva, Skira, 1990 (2nd edition).
- Boorstin D., *Les Créateurs*, Paris, Seghers, 1994.
- Cabane P., *Harmenszoon van Rijin Rembrandt*, Paris, Le Chêne, 1991.
- Cachin F., *Gauguin*, Paris, Flammarion, 2003.
- Comte-Sponville A., *Chardin, ou la matière heureuse*, Paris, Adam Biro, 1999.
- Huygue R., *Dialogue avec le visible*, Paris, Flammarion, 1955.
- Jobert B., *Delacriox*, Paris, Gallimard, 1997.
- Kilmuray E., Ormond R., *Sargent*, London, Tate Gallery Publications, 1998.
- Marijnissen R.H. *et al.*, *Bruegel*, Paris, Mercatorfonds and Éditions Charles Moreau, 2003.
- Montias J.M., Blankert A., Aillaud G., *Vermeer*, Paris, Hazan, 2004 (2nd edition).
- Ragon M., *Gustave Courbet, peintre de la liberté*, Paris, Fayard, 2004.
- Rosenblum, R., *Les Peintures au Musée d'Orsay*, Paris, La Martinière, 1995.
- Sala C., *Caspar Friedrich et la peinture romantique*, Paris, Éditions Pierre Terrail, 1993.
- Terrasse A., *Bonnard 'La couleur agit'*, Paris, Découvertes series, Gallimard, 1999.
- Thuillier J., *Fragonard*, Geneva, Skira, 1987.
- Venturi L., *La Peinture de la Renaissance. De Bruegel au Greco*, Geneva, Skira, 1979.
- Vigouroux R., *La Fabrique du beau*, Paris, Odile Jacob, 1992.
- Walter I.F., Metzger R., *Vincent Van Gogh, the complete paintings*, Cologne, Taschen, 2012.
- Wildenstein D., *Monet or the Triumph of Impressionism*, Cologne, Taschen, 2013.
- Wittkower R. and M., *Les Enfants de Saturne: psychologie et comportement des artistes de l'Antiquité à la Révolution française*, Paris, Macula, 1991.
- Zeki S., *Inner Vision: an exploration of art and brain*, Oxford, Oxford University Press, 1999.

MINDFULNESS

25 ways to live in the moment through art

Christophe André

Illustrated in full colour throughout, this bestselling book draws upon art as a source of inspiration. With stunning simplicity and clarity, mindfulness expert Christophe André sets out 25 life-changing lessons – from understanding what it means to live mindfully, to using mindfulness in everyday situations.

Poetic yet practical, essential for the journey of life, here is a beautiful book to return to again and again.

ISBN 978 1846044632

Order direct from www.penguin.co.uk